D1560251

Posthumous Diary

EUGENIO MONTALE

Posthumous Diary

[Diario postumo]

TRANSLATED FROM THE ITALIAN AND
ANNOTATED BY *Jonathan Galassi*

TURTLE POINT PRESS : NEW YORK : 2001

© Arnoldo Mondadori Editore SpA

Introduction and translation
© 2001 by Jonathan Galassi

LCCN 00-136361
ISBN 1-885586-22-1

Design and composition by
Wilsted & Taylor Publishing Services

CONTENTS

ANOTHER MONTALE

lasciate in pace i vivi per rinvivire
i morti: nell'aldilà mi voglio divertire.

—"Secondo testamento"

*A*nother Montale? We know the anguished, increasingly vatic poet of the great "first" period—*Ossi di seppia* (1925), *Le occasioni* (1939), and *La bufera e altro* (1956) —the anti-D'Annunzian, "hermetic" neo-stilnovist who gave voice to doubt, negation, and hopeless love in a hard, relentless rhetoric that was definitive for twentieth-century Italian poetry. And we know the resigned, self-ironizing "second" Montale, the poet of the other side of the medal or "back of the shop," the poet-as-critic who commented on his first three canticles in the voluminous work of his last two decades: *Satura* (1971), *Diario del '71 e del '72* (1973), *Quaderno di quattro anni* (1977), *Altri versi* (1981). We know, too, the humor, the legerdemain, the urbane common sense of Montale the prose writer, the journalist and author of *terza pagina* think pieces, stories, and literary, music, art, and cultural criticism in numerous distinctive moods and tones. All these Montales are familiar, and if they're not, Mondadori's multi-volume Meridiani edition makes them readily available, more than six thousand pages' worth. Still, in the twenty years since Montale's death in 1981, new facets of this protean figure have begun to emerge, and no doubt there are others yet to be uncovered—the caustic epigrammatist, for one, virtuoso practitioner of an ancient and ongoing tradition, whose malicious bons mots remain the jealously guarded property, for the most part, of privileged friends and associates.

Unsurprisingly, considering the deep, dark shadow that the poet's work has cast over Italian letters, Montale has endured a series of posthumous *ad hominem* attacks. It has been revealed, for instance, that many of his translations from English and other languages were penned with the silent collaboration of his friend Lucia Morpurgo Rodocanachi. It has been revealed that he employed the American poet and D'Annunzio cohort Henry Furst to write reviews of English and American books, which Montale, in observance of time-honored Italian practice, subsequently revised and published under his own name. Nasty stories abound, too, about purported snobberies, pettinesses, and minor cruelties—all very much in keeping with the latter-day reconfiguration of a dominant artist's profile. Indeed, one might well say that the "scandals" that have surfaced, and the relish with which they have been seized upon, offer a highly reliable gauge of Montale's continuing potency and relevance: as our view of him becomes ever more complicated and nuanced, he grows ever more fascinating.

One of the notable "new" Montales of recent years is the literary gamesman, the *poète en pantoufles* amusing himself in elaborate *jeux d'esprit*, playing tricks on his faithful courtiers as well as his enemies and competitors and whipping boys of choice, the critics. We've seen evidence of this before, in Montale's occasionally obfuscatory or even deliberately misleading responses to intrusive or hamfisted critical inquiry. In "Il *tu*," the introductory poem to *Sa-*

tura, he speaks of his critics as "depistati," thrown off course, by the multiple personae to whom his poems are addressed, and it's clear that the poet enjoyed keeping ahead of the hermeneutical pack, sending them off in misleading directions (though he also clearly enjoyed being chased).

The book at hand, known as the *Diario postumo*, has been presented as Montale's eighth and final collection of poems, but it is something else as well: an elaborate and spectacular collaboration, an intricate literary game which, as the poet himself predicted, gave rise to a "firestorm" of proportions unprecedented in the annals of modern Italian literature. Whether the still-unresolved controversy it aroused was in itself part of the poet's intention only adds to its mystery.

The *Diario postumo* consists of eighty-four poems written for Annalisa Cima, a Milanese poet and artist with whom Montale became acquainted in 1968. He was then in his early seventies, while Cima, a beautiful and spirited woman of means, was in her late twenties. She often kept him company in his later years, particularly after his retirement from the *Corriere della Sera* in 1973, and their relationship lasted until his death in 1981. Cima herself published a brief impressionistic account of her friendship with the poet, *Incontro Montale*, in 1973, and in 1977 she and the critic Cesare Segre co-edited an academic anthology, *Eugenio Montale: Profilo di un autore*. In 1978, Cima established the Schlesinger Foundation, named for her maternal great-grandmother, who came from a family of Viennese bankers, for the promotion of artistic projects in which she was interested; Montale served as its honorary president until his death.

As Cima tells it,[1] Montale conceived of the *Diario* as a project meant to help exorcize his fear of mortality, in which she participated as faithful disciple, collaborator, and enabler, assisting him in creating a secret last book that would appear in installments after his death. Starting in 1969, Montale, each time they met, would present her with a poem he had written for her. In 1979, he decided to divide the compositions, written over eleven years, into eleven envelopes: ten of these, numbered I to X, contained six poems each, while a larger, unnumbered eleventh packet held another envelope of six (number XI), as well as a packet of eighteen additional poems for three more "virtual" envelopes. The poems were entrusted to Cima with the understanding that they were not to be published during Montale's lifetime. Five years after his death, the Schlesinger Foundation began issuing a series of annual *plaquettes*, numbered I to XI, one for each grouping of six poems, in a private, limited edition. A twelfth volume, containing the additional eighteen texts, was printed in 1996, the same year that Mondadori published a trade edition of the entire diary, its title decided by Cima (Mondadori had brought out the first thirty poems in a 1991 volume).

In July 1997, Dante Isella, a leading philologist, who had known Montale and who has published an edition of *Le occasioni*, wrote in the *Corriere della Sera*, Montale's old newspaper, that the *Diario postumo* was, as he put it, "apocryphal," claiming that it had been constructed by its dedicatee out of "snippets of phrases taken from oral conversations with the poet . . . phrases that survived either in

1. in her introductory note to the *Diario postumo*.

xii

her memory or on tape, which were then strung together"[2] using a "patchwork" poetic technique.

The response was the firestorm that Montale had perhaps been hoping for. Scores of articles appeared in every kind of publication, with many leading critics and poets taking sides. Some claimed that Isella had acted out of resentment at having been denied the opportunity to edit Montale's collected poems. Others, angry that they had not been in on the poet's game, denied it could possibly be true. The question of the authenticity of the texts seemed to be definitively laid to rest when Maria Corti, the curator of the manuscript collection at the University of Pavia, to which Montale had donated the bulk of his papers, revealed that Montale had long ago told her about the poems and the practical joke he intended to perpetrate on his critics.[3] After Isella further questioned the authenticity of the manuscripts, Cima mounted an exhibition of them in Lugano that October; the publisher Vanni Scheiwiller issued the acts of the attendant seminar, with contributions by numerous respected *montalisti*, the following year. Cima also produced the so-called "Swiss will," a 1979 document in which Montale names her as the heir of his entire literary corpus. This was contested by the poet's niece, Bianca Montale, professor of Italian history at the University of Genova, who was the executrix of an earlier will. Cima has not further pressed her claim to control Montale's entire body of work, but the polemics continue to this day.

2. Isella's articles have been collected in a small book, *Dovuto a Montale* (Milan: Archinto, 1997); the quotation appears on p. 15.

3. See Maria Corti, "La storia lontana del *Diario postumo*," in *Atti del seminario sul Diario postumo di Eugenio Montale. Lugano, 24–26 October 1997*. Milan: All'Insegna del Pesce d'Oro, 1999, 42–45.

To this reader, the posthumous diary is clearly a Montalean text—though a very different (and diminished) one from the so-called diary poems of the last collections published in the poet's lifetime. How to account for the undeniable falling-off from the sinuous aphoristic concentration and rhythmic elegance, the precise vocabulary, the exquisitely distilled quality of the late poems, in these looser, flatter, more tentative and fragmentary compositions written at the same time?

First, the differences are not absolute. Though the late canonical poems have a linguistic and intellectual finesse that the posthumous ones don't generally approach, there are moments where the poet's two voices, public and private, are notably convergent. What is evident about the *Diario postumo* is that it represents an instance virtually unique in Montale's work of truly unpremeditated, unmediated private poetry. These are not the aphoristic philosophical meditations, interspersed with occasional longer verse portraits, that make up the published "notebooks," all of them preoccupied with the emptiness of the present, the intermittence of the past, and the imminence of death—and, I would contend, contrary to Montale's own claims, strenuously worked over.[4] The posthumous poems are literally occasional texts, jotted down off the cuff on whatever material was available in anticipation of the arrival of his friend and fellow conspirator and later (possibly with her collaboration) only minimally revised. They are the artifacts of a game; but they are also the raw

4. For a revealing example of how a draft of a Montale poem can diverge significantly from the canonical text, see the original version of the acrostic poem for Marialuisa Spaziani, "Da un lago svizzero," published in *Il Giorno* (8 April 1997) and reproduced in E.M. *Collected Poems 1920–1954*, tr. Jonathan Galassi, 605.

material, the primary stuff of Montale's poetry—they make the same gestures as the published poems, if often in a rudimentary, formulaic manner, and they echo and rehearse the poet's lifelong preoccupations, as Montale's late work continually does, to the point of quoting or paraphrasing some of the poet's best-known lines and tropes. Here, yet again, is another songbook dedicated to one more presiding muse, one more "daughter of light"—this time the beautiful and beguiling young friend whose presence enables him to re-invoke and rehearse yet again the time-honored gestures of his poetry, standing in for Clizia, Volpe, Annetta, and the other prime engendering figures of his imagination. Here, too, are the aged poet's enduring preoccupations with illusion and the limits of belief, with seen and unseen worlds (so much so that a book-length study[5] has been devoted to the gnostic subtext of the *Diario postumo*). But the poems are not only about solitude and despair and the fear of death; they are also about those things that alleviate existential loneliness: the friendship that comes of shared interests and beliefs, and the consolations of art, including the notional immortality it can sometimes offer.

Many of the posthumous poems are concerned with issues of poetic paternity (and maternity), with the handing on of values, the custody of a mortally endangered heritage, and the survival of the poetic self in the work of others—themes that rarely reach the surface in Montale's canonical work (though anxiety about the survival of his poetry is a lifelong preoccupation), but which resonate tellingly here, being natural concomitants of an intimate grappling with death and dissolution. The texts, given

---

5. by Paolo De Caro. See the bibliography.

their occasional, on-the-fly character, are often sketchy in themselves, insolent-seeming, even, in their disregard for the work of poem-making to which Montale assiduously devoted himself; yet taken as a whole, they embody the obverse of the Montalean medal, the back of the mortality shop, in which the poet gives voice not only to his fears, but to his hopes, dreams, and needs. Another Montale, then—playing fast and loose with the poetry game, deriding its handlers and usurpers; yet also gentler, more open, more intimate and forgiving, more avuncular, or, even, parental: the poet of the *plazer*, the wish-fulfilling dream, who celebrates the comfort that the attention of a beautiful and devoted friend offers to an old man on the theshold of annihilation.

And then, beyond the poems themselves, there is the game, the "scandal" which the poet of negation plotted to leave behind, speaking from the grave, as it were, and preventing the critics from comfortably settling his posthumous reputation. Giuseppe Marcenaro has written that a "poetic gesture" like the one perpetrated by Montale "represents the eclipse of literature itself."[6] Montale's friend and fellow poet Andrea Zanzotto expressed much the same notion when he wrote of the "idea of auto-demolition" that seems to prevail in many of the poems of the *Diario postumo* "as if he wished to denigrate himself,"[7] pre-empting the critics through self-criticism and

6. Giuseppe Marcenaro, *Eugenio Montale*. Milan: Bruno Mondadori, 1999, 106.

7. Quoted in Corti, 45. See also Zanzotto's "Testimonianza," in the *Atti del seminario sul Diario postumo*, 157–162, in which he refers (158) to the Diario as the "(very serious) joke of a *revenant*, a ghost, who would come to disturb our incessantly reordered literary cards with the preordained scansion of his own "posthumous poetry." Zanzotto adds

self-diminishment, while Maria Corti called this last aspect of Montale's work "a phase of desacralization, of parodistic play."[8] It is as if the secretive scribbling of a last new ghost of a songbook, this wilfully sketchy, ironic reprise, carefully planned to emerge stealthily well after his death, represented a defiant refusal to accept the mummification imposed by a cultural system that had allotted him a fixed, albeit central place of honor; indeed, his insistence on upsetting the terms of his own reception are reminiscent in certain respects of his willed redefinition of the language of the Italian lyric at the beginning of his career. The outrage and excitement, the plaquettes and articles, theses and exegeses, the debates, conferences, lawsuits, concordances, apparatuses, dissertations, and translations—what better commentary on the alienating superstructure to which literature is subjected in the information age? Who's kidding whom? Montale asks, as we fall into his trap.

But perhaps the joke is on Montale, finally—for the fact remains that the *Diario postumo*, calculatedly offhand as it is, still has the power to move us, all in all; the poems, which to some enact the end of poetry itself, nevertheless glow intermittently with the faint yet intense radioactivity of art. In the end all the Montales, like all his *tu*s, all his muses, are one and the same: everything he touches, even at his most willfully nugatory, is hopelessly freighted with significance, more so even than its creator himself may have always recognized. This new, premedi-

(his emphasis), "*I think Montale could not resist the thought of making his own apocrypha, here, literally, etymologically understood as 'hidden writing' precisely because it is excluded from any sort of canon, into a kind of mise-en-abîme of all his previous work.*"

8. Corti, 45.

tated anti-finale to his work not only manages to under-
line our appreciation for what preceded it, as it goes one
last time through the deeply-etched motions of Montalean
meaning-making; it also pulses with its own tenuous yet
undeniable life as it casts its blue light out and backward
and forward.

—J.G.

Posthumous Diary

Se la mosca ti avesse vista
anche una sola volta
quanto amore ti avrebbe
accordato. Non è facile
per me dare se non
            per interposta persona,
cosa direbbe la Gina
se decidessi d'essere
padre all'improvviso.

If The Fly had seen you
even once
how much love she would have
granted you. Giving
isn't easy for me
        except through third persons—
what would Gina say
if I decided suddenly
to be a father.

La tua età m'impaura
ti difende e m'accusa.
Ignori il vento dell'affanno
col suo fardello, ma ti sorvola
il favore d'una musa che ritrovo
sul volto. A caso tradurremo
domani qualche verso di Emily
insieme. E verrai col tuo
muflone blu cobalto.
Anima viva, sai dare vita
a me che ignoro e brancolo
in un tempo che vola
come i tuoi trent'anni.

Your age frightens me
protects you and indicts me.
You don't know the wind of anguish
and its burden, but the favor
of a muse I can see in your face
watches over you. Maybe tomorrow
we'll translate a few lines of Emily
together. And you'll come
with your cobalt blue mouflon.
Living spirit, you know how
to give me life, who feel my way
in a time that flies
like your thirty years.

Quando sarai imperatrice
due amici contenderanno
il tuo fianco
in veste di ministri-consiglieri.
Ma nulla torna
se non il rombo lumeggiante
dei motori.
Mi sorprende la vita stessa
in quest'ora, amica
l'ala del destino ignora se tra
gli assenti noi saremo insieme.

When you are empress
two friends will vie
to stand at your side
as your minister-counselors.
But nothing returns
but the echoing
rumble of motors.
Life itself surprises me
in this moment, friend,
the wing of destiny can't know if you and I
will be together among the absent.

Agile messaggero eccoti
tendo esitante la lettera per
Adelheit.

L'insensato cantore si ritira
rimbalza a te la palla
che decide la sorte.

Si trattò forse d'una allucinazione?
o fu l'ammaliatrice
solo un'apparizione

a cui non seppi opporre
altro diniego che la fuga.
Corri da lei, Agrodolce

e torna dall'esausto genearca
con un ricordo lieto.
Un gesto che

regali l'eliso: questo mi basta,
così impervio è il cammino tracciato
dagli iddii a noi mortali.

Agile messenger, here you are
hesitant I hold the letter for
Adelheit.

The foolish bard withdraws,
the ball that decides his fate
falls in your court.

Maybe it was an hallucination?
or was the sorceress
simply an apparition

to which I could offer
no other rebuttal than flight?
Run to her, Bittersweet,

and bring back your worn-out forebear
a happy souvenir.
A gesture

that bestows Elysium: it's all I need,
so arduous is the pathway traced
by the gods for us mortals.

È SOLO UN VIZIO

Fliaci travestiti da poeti
burocrati arroganti,
pedanti imbonitori
siete voi i vessilliferi:
portatori d'insegne sbiadite.
L'esser poeti non è un vanto.
È solo un vizio di natura.
Un peso che s'ingroppa
con paura.

Clowns disguised as poets,
arrogant bureacrats,
pedantic criers
you're the standard bearers:
carrying faded colors.
Being a poet isn't a matter of pride.
It's only an error of nature.
A burden to be shouldered
with fear.

EX ABRUPTO

Uno spazio di anni ci separa,
ma rapido un tuo gesto
annulla la distanza.
Fuoriesce un libricino
dal magazzino di una grossa borsa,
e limpido risuona un verso
che devo giudicare.
È il saperti uguale
in un tempo diverso che forse
m'addolora. Una lieve brezza
tra barbagli di luce solleva
nugoli di sabbia e spume. E
ciò che viene a galla ex abrupto
è ch'io sono la musa e tu il cantore.
Notizia lieta, sentirsi al tempo stesso
maestro e ispiratore.
Il vate è morto, evviva l'estintore.

A space of years divides us
but suddenly a gesture
of yours annuls the distance.
A little book emerges
out of the storehouse of a giant purse
and a limpid line reverberates
that I must judge.
It's knowing you're the same
in a different time
that saddens me, perhaps. A little breeze
between light flashes stirs up
clouds of sand and foam. And
what surfaces ex abrupto
is that I'm the muse and you the poet.
Happy news, to feel at once
both master and instigator.
The bard is dead, long live his terminator.

MATTINATA

Sulla porta si profila
un'aerea figura.
Eccoti col girasole
delle tue aureole.
Né alcuna presenza potrà
turbare questa gaiezza
che ci riproponi.

Ad ogni apparizione
fai rifiorire vegetazioni nuove.
Non hai un cliché:
emergi singolare. È il segno
che travalica gli umani.
A noi, in questo anfiteatro
di brutture, non resta
che ricordo e dulia
qual duplice ristoro.

An airy figure
looms in the doorway.
Here you are, with the sunflower
of your halo-curls.
Nor can any presence
disturb this gaiety
you offer us anew.

At every apparition
you make new vegetation flower.
You have no label:
you emerge unique. It's the sign
that transcends human knowing.
For us, in this amphitheatre
of ugliness, only
memory and veneration survive
as a double refreshment.

No non t'allontanare
mio guerriero.
Lungo il percorso
che conduce alla foce
il vento furioso
scuote i vecchi rami.
E a ogni soffio di gelo
tremano i fogliami.
A volte, pavento nel silenzio
che arrivi la mannara
e tronchi ogni esitare.
Ma s'attenua il timore
nell'attesa . . .
che mi è più familiare.

No, don't go
my warrior.
Along the path
that leads to the rivermouth
the raging wind
beats the old branches.
And at every icy gust
the hard leaves tremble.
Sometimes in the silence I'm afraid
the ax will arrive
and cut short all hesitation.
But my fear abates
in the waiting. . . .
which is more familiar.

MA C'È CHI

Potius mori quam foedari
è l'illibato senso
del vivere che trasmetti
in messaggi cifrati.
Ma c'è chi non capisce
e preferisce il mondo
così com'è: immerso in un pattume.

Potius mori quam foedari
is the unsullied sense
of living you transmit
in coded messages.
But there are those who don't understand
and prefer the world
the way it is: buried in garbage.

Certo le Parche han filato
lo stame e addugliano
i cavi delle nostre vite.
Ma dei confini tra finito
e infinito, e dello spazio
che ci separa dal baratro,
non ne sappiamo niente.
Siamo dentro un involucro
serrati fino al collo
e nulla torna, se non forse
il ricordo. Il clou
non è quaggiù—tu dici—
è il prosieguo, l'eterno,
v'è metamorfosi non metempsicosi.
Ratio ultima rerum . . . id est deus.
E fu così che il tuo parlare
timoroso e ardente, mi rese
in breve da ateo credente.

Surely the Fates have spun
their thread and are winding
the lines of our lives.
But of the boundaries between finite
and infinite, or the space
that keeps us from the abyss,
we know nothing.
We're sealed in an envelope
up to our necks
and nothing returns, except maybe
memory. The gist—you say—
isn't down here,
it's the sequel, the eternal,
there's metamorphosis not metempsychosis.
Ratio ultima rerum . . . id est deus.
And so your hesitant, ardent
words soon turned me
from atheist into believer.

DIE FLEDERMAUS

Indugi sulla porta nell'entrare,
sei come uno smarrito adolescente.
Con una aureola di cerchietti
fumiganti—ti circonfondo.
Oggi siamo ambedue convalescenti
faremo un nouveau jeu:
canterò un brano che dovrai indovinare:
Fa re mi mi sol.
Il titolo, il titolo, su presto.
La vedo un po' confusa
balbetta qualche cosa.
Poi tutto d'un fiato: il pipistrello.
Signora mi dispiace,
il tempo consentito è già passato.

You hang back at the doorway coming in,
like a lost adolescent.
With a halo of smoky curls
I enfold you.
Today we're both recuperating
we'll play a new game:
I'll sing a passage and you'll have to guess:
Fa re mi mi sol.
The name, the name, come on!
She looks a bit confused
and mumbles something.
Then suddenly: The bat.
Sorry, ma'am,
time's up.

L'inafferrabile tua amica scrive
e poi dilegua, sta per arrivare
ed è di nuovo . . . assente.
Il dubbio è che non sia
se non nella tua mente.
Eppure ho un nebuloso ricordo di lei.
Mi prometti una sua visita
da mesi. Ma *la critica*
non mostra il suo sembiante:
che sia una estravagante
danzatrice di parole.
Oppure quel suo nome che muove
da incertezza e finisce in risa
è la chiave di tutto il suo mistero.
La chiameremo a gran voce sull'aria
del ben noto Milanese, con sottofondo
di corno-inglese. E a simile richiamo
certo l'inafferrabile apparirà
                              improvvisa.

Your elusive friend writes,
then vanishes, is about to arrive
and then again is . . . not.
The question is whether she exists
except in your mind.
Yet I have a hazy memory of her.
You've promised me she'll visit me
for months. But *the critic*
doesn't show her face:
maybe she's an eccentric
dancer of words.
Or it's her name, which starts
in doubt and ends in merriment,
that is the key to all her mystery.
We'll call her, bellowing
the famous Milanese's aria, with undertone
of English horn. And at such a summons
surely the elusive one will appear
                              out of thin air.

Noi non abbiamo cognizione
della futurizione.
La nostra previsione è limitata.
Quanto al libero arbitrio
farei qualche eccezione.
Non vi è biforcazione, ma
percorso obbligato.

We have no security
about futurity.
Our foresight's limited.
As to free will
I have a few objections.
There's no bifurcation, it's all
one way.

La congettura che il mondo
sia una burla, anch'essa
non risolve il puzzle fondamentale.
Se vuoi la mia opinione
l'unica via d'uscita è l'illusione,
perché ogni giorno la vita
supera il limite che pone.

Even the supposition that the world's
a hoax
doesn't solve the fundamental puzzle.
If you want my opinion,
illusion is the one way out,
since every day life supersedes
the limit that it sets.

Ed ecco, nel tentativo maldestro
di spiegare ogni possibile significato
il fine dicitore è naufragato
sulle spiagge stranote del banale.

Che vuoi che importi a un grullo ascoltatore
d'essere un eone decaduto o un uomo
che per paura è diventato muto.

And here, in the maladroit attempt
to expound every possible meaning
the eloquent orator founders
on the famed shores of the banal.

What should it matter to a dimwit listener
if he's a fallen being or a man
gone mute out of fear.

Un grande ombrello d'ombre
che or rotonde ora oblunghe
decidono il mezzogiorno o l'imbrunire.
Sere e tramonti rosa, in questo
inusuale salotto, dove ho visto
sfilare le tue amiche. Paola
la bruna dagli occhi smeraldo
verrà ancora?

A great umbrella of shadows,
now circles, now ellipses,
decides between midday and dusk.
Pink evenings and pink sunsets, in this
unusual salon, where I've watched
your friends file past. Will Paola
the brunette with the emerald eyes
be coming again?

NEL GIARDINO

Discendi dal gran viale
e ti sovrasta un cielo
azzurro estivo. Una nuvola
bianca di lini rinfresca
la canicola al tuo arrivo.
Ci sediamo sulla solita panchina.
Poi d'un tratto un soffio di vento
e la tua paglia comincia a turbinare.
L'afferri, ti risiedi.
L'ala del grande pino marino
come vela spiegata ci trascina.
Vorremmo bordeggiare
da questo litorale tutta la costiera,
giungere in un duetto di nomi, di ricordi
fino a Nervi.
Ma il sole già declina,
diffonde il suo lucore in raggi obliqui,
dispare, torna, e la memoria di sere
uguali raddoppia gli orizzonti,
traduce in altri giorni
quel momento fugace che scompare.
Ora anche il vento tace.

You descend from the wide avenue
crowned by an azure
summer sky. A white
linen cloud relieves
the heat with your arrival.
We sit on the usual bench.
Then a sudden gust of wind
and your straw hat starts to spin.
You grab it, sit back down.
The wing of the tall sea pine
pulls us like a spread sail.
We'd like to tack from this beach
all the way down the coast
to Nervi in a duet
of names and memories.
But the sun's already setting,
diffusing its splendor in slant rays,
it disappears, returns, and the thought
of evenings like these redoubles the horizons,
transports the fleeting moment
that fades into other days.
Now the wind, too, is silent.

RICORDO

Lei sola percepiva i suoni
dei miei silenzi. Temevo
a volte che fuggisse il tempo
ostile mentre parlavamo.
Dopodiché ho smarrito la memoria
ed ora mi ritrovo a parlare
di lei con te, tra spirali di fumo
che velano la nostra commozione.
Ed è questa la parte di me che ritrovo
mutata: il sentimento, per sé informe,
in quest'oggi che è solo di rimpianto.

Only she perceived the sounds
in my silences. Now and then
I was afraid that hostile
time would flee while we talked.
After which I lost my memory
and now I find myself talking
of her with you, among smoke
spirals that veil our emotion.
It's this, the part of me I find
transformed: a feeling, shapeless in itself,
in this now that is only regret.

Eravamo indecisi tra
esultanza e paura
alla notizia che il *computer*
rimpiazzerà la penna del poeta.
Nel caso personale, non sapendolo
usare, ripiegherò su schede,
che attingano ai ricordi
per poi riunirle a caso.
Ed ora che m'importa
se la vena si smorza
insieme a me sta finendo un'era.

We were undecided
between exulting and fear
at the news the computer
will replace the poet's pen.
In my case, not knowing
how to use it, I'll depend
on notecards drawn from memory,
and shuffle them at random.
But what does it matter now
if the gift is dying out—
an age is ending with me.

Ogni giorno c'è una rivoluzione
di stagioni, di popoli, di idee.
Sine die è rimandata ogni decisione.
Nulla è più stabile, se non qualche canzone
ripetuta sotto tutte le bandiere.
Quanto si salverà, da questo nubifragio,
non si sa. Forse dopo tanto spreco
anche la parola finirà in un botro.
A noi rimane la speranza che qualche
anacoreta distilli resine dorate
dai tronchi marcescenti del sapere.

There's a revolution every day
in seasons, peoples, and ideas.
All decision's put off *sine die*.
Nothing's stable anymore, except
a few songs that get played under every flag.
What will survive from this downpour
no one knows. Perhaps after so much waste
the word itself will end up in a ditch.
What's left for us is the hope
that a few anchorites will distil golden resins
from the rotting trunks of wisdom.

INCONTRO

Esitammo un istante,
e dopo poco riconoscemmo
di avere la stessa malattia.
Non vi è definizione
per questa mirabile tortura,
c'è chi la chiama *spleen*
e chi malinconia.
Ma se accettiamo il gioco
ai margini troviamo
un segno intelleggibile
che può dar senso al tutto.

We hesitated an instant,
then soon we understood
we had the same disease.
There's no definition
for this sublime torture,
some call it *spleen*,
others melancholy.
But if we accept the game
at the side we find
a legible sign
that may give it all meaning.

Non so se un testamento in bilico
tra prosa e poesia vincerà il niente
di ciò che sopravvive.
L'oracolare tono della versificazione
non cadrà nell'indifferenza
e un brandello, una parte della mia
impotenza farà vendetta del prima
e dell'ignoto. Non scelsi mai la strada
più battuta, ma accettai il fato
nel suo inganno di sempre.
Ed ora che s'approssima la fine getto
la mia bottiglia che forse darà luogo
a un vero parapiglia.
Non vi è mai stato un nulla in cui sparire
già altri grazie al ricordo son risorti,
lasciate in pace i vivi per rinvivire
i morti: nell'aldilà mi voglio divertire.

I don't know if a testament halfway
between prose and poetry will overcome
the nothing of what survives.
The oracular tone of the verse
won't meet with indifference
and a sliver, a part of my impotence
will vindicate the earlier
and the unknown. I never took the road
more traveled, but accepted fate
in its usual deceit.
And now that the end is nearing I'm tossing
my bottle which may well give rise
to a real firestorm.
There's never been a nothingness to hide in,
already others have returned by way of memory,
leave the living in peace to revive the dead:
I want to enjoy myself in the beyond.

Quando lo nominasti la prima volta
pensai alle Fagacee.
Ne parlavi con accenti intenti
sogguardando le mie reazioni,
poi sfilasti con *fair play*
un libro di traduzioni.
Fu solo la paura di dover giudicare
di farmi giudicare che impedì
di fissare il nuovo incontro.
Persi così, dicesti, un animo speciale
una figura uscita da un quadro di El Greco.
A me, certo, bastò quel tuo slancio amicale.

The first time you said his name
I thought of the Fagaceae.
You spoke about him earnestly,
eyeing my reactions,
then pulled out, in the spirit of "fair play,"
a book of his translations.
It was only the fear of having to judge,
of being judged, that kept me
from fixing our next meeting.
And so I missed, you said, a special spirit,
a figure out of a painting by El Greco.
For me, your friendly onslaught was enough.

47

COME MADRE

La luce che diffonde il Monte Amiata
quando il sole declina,
la folata di vento che dall'orizzonte
s'avvicina: questo vorremmo possedere.
Ma ora afflitti dal ritmo quotidiano
ora incupiti dal senso di colpa
viviamo come trote avviluppate nella mota.
Poi, a fior d'acqua, la visione lieta
d'una scia d'opale che in pochi istanti stinge
lasciando un solco per farsi ricordare.
Ed è la prova che mi consola. Un giorno
anch'io sarò alvo per chi non mi smemora.

The light Mount Amiata emanates
as the sun goes down,
the gust of wind that nears from the horizon:
these we would like to own.
But now afflicted by our daily rhythm
now weighed down by the sense of sin
we live like trout enshrouded in mud.
Then, on the water's surface, the happy vision
of an opal streak that fades in a few seconds
leaving a wake to be remembered by.
And it's this proof that consoles me. One day I, too,
will be a womb for those who won't forget me.

Ieri sentii che l'inverno mi aveva
riservata una sorpresa lieta.
Svelavi ad alta voce i miei pensieri.
—E se la vita fosse un mistero vano?
—Resta nel tuo eliso, non essere crudele
verso quel vago senso di speranza
che a noi, solo, rimane. Ben altro
è la felicità. Esiste, forse,
ma non la conosciamo.

Yesterday I understood that winter
had saved a glad surprise for me.
You spoke my thoughts aloud.
—And if life were an empty mystery?
—Stay in your heaven, don't be cruel
to the vague sense of hope
which is all that's left for us. Happiness
is something else. It exists, perhaps,
but we don't know it.

L'INSONNIA

L'insonnia, che è incastro di ombre
e lucori, trasformerà le voci
in sgomento. Più tardi i suoni
si fonderanno, radi, al buio della notte.
Il tempo correrà a rilento verso l'albeggiare.
Poi l'angoscia limbale disparirà
in un giorno che si spera migliore.

Insomnia, interlocking
shadow and shine, will turn the voices
into terror. Later the intermittent sounds
will blend, dispersed, into the dark of night.
Slowly time will flow toward dawn.
Then the limbal anguish will vanish
in a day one hopes will be better.

L'estate è scossa da forti temporali.
Le nubi si rincorrono lungo la riviera.
I giorni sono in fuga sempre uguali.
Ma all'improvviso lo spettacolo muta.
Lontano, grigio e livido, il fumo
di una petroliera appare e si dissolve
lieve in un arcobaleno.

Summer is shaken by strong storms.
Clouds chase themselves along the shore.
The days are fleeting, every one the same.
But suddenly the show has changed.
Far off, gray and livid, smoke
from a tanker appears and softly
dissolves in a rainbow.

HONORIS CAUSA

Pensano i mini-professori
che per poetare
occorre essere laureati.
E le generazioni future
vedranno il guasto
di tali affermazioni.
Si dirà: fu buon poeta
perché ebbe la laurea
a titolo d'onore.

The mini-professors think
one needs a degree
to write poetry.
Coming generations
will see the foolishness
of such assertions.
They'll say: he was a good poet
because he won the laurel crown
of honor.

INCERTEZZE

Nella scelta del mese più adatto
a lunghi viaggi immaginari, indugiavamo
tra maggio salvato dall'arrivo dell'estate
e settembre che non è disperato,
ma neppur lieto. Aprile lo lasciammo
ad altri recensori. Fummo dell'opinione
di trascurare i mesi uccisi dalla morsa del gelo.
Così il tempo inesorabile scorre
e improvviso, d'un balzo, s'arresta.

Choosing the best month
for long imaginary journeys, we delayed
between May, saved by summer's arrival,
and September, not despairing,
but not joyous either. April we left
to other reviewers. We agreed
to skip the months killed off by frost.
So flows inexorable time
and suddenly, with a start, comes to a halt.

L'INVESTITURA

Non so se fu la sua Beltà a sommuovere
la tua ammirazione. Lo designasti
senza ambiguità divenne il Serenissimo
dopo una fumata. Ammesso a far parte
dell'olimpo, in segno d'elezione,
fu da quel giorno il nome ricorrente
in tante discussioni. Lo rileggevamo.
E le parole rimbalzavan tra noi
aligere faville sfuggite dal profondo
bruno color della pietra focaia.
Come limpida finì quella giornata
nel ricordo è ancora viva.
Quando varcherò il confine designato
il vostro *hochetus* alla memoria
eluderà gli abissi di silenzio?

I don't know if it was his *Beltà* that aroused
your admiration. You designated him
without ambiguity, he became *il Serenissimo*
with a smoke signal. Once admitted
to Olympus, as a sign of his election
his name recurred from that day on
in countless discussions. We re-read him.
And words ricocheted between us
winged sparks escaping
from the deep brown, color of flint.
How bright that day's end was
still lives in memory.
When I cross the designated border
will your *hochetus* in my memory
elude the abysses of silence?

Nella grande New York: caput mundi
incontrerai: Marianne, Djuna ed anche
il re della baia. Il gentleman
che scrive poco—virtù oggi assai rara.
C'è nel suo stile asciutto il sapere
di ricordi, orgogliosamente conservati
e mai consunti.

In great big New York, caput mundi,
you'll meet: Marianne, Djuna and also
the king of the bay. The gentleman
who writes little—virtue very rare today.
In his dry style is the wisdom
of memories jealously guarded
and never spent.

L'ESEGETA

Il nostro falansterio sarà più singolare
di quello di Fourier, in un'esedra
musici suoneranno dal risveglio
sino a sera. Il Sommo sarà
ammesso, senza esitazioni
gli altri dovranno sottoporsi ad una
votazione. Se l'empirismo logico
ci vieta di credere che può essere
valida una tale fantasia,
non abbiamo altra scelta per poter
dare un volto a questa autentica follia.

Our phalanstery will be more singular
than Fourier's, on a portico
musicians will perform
from waking
till evening. The Highest will be
let in, without hesitation,
the others will have to be put
to a vote. If logical empiricism
won't allow us to believe
in the truth of such a fantasy,
we have no other way to give a face
to this authentic folly.

A sufficenza ne abbiamo di un mondo
che già scoppia. Rumori di motori
sculture fatte a strati, libri
che s'ammucchiano su tutti gli scaffali.
La raffica c'investe, induce ad acquistare
fin l'ultimo giornale. Poi tutto brucerà
dans l'espace d'un matin. Ignoro
quali sventure porterà con sé
il trionfo del caduco e se
si salveranno poche parole imperiture.

We're fed up with a world
that's exploding already. Running motors
sculptures in layers, books
piling up on all the shelves.
The squall assails us, tempting us to buy
down to the last paper. Then everything will burn
dans l'espace d'un matin. I don't know
what mishaps the triumph of the transitory
will entail, or whether
a few immortal words will be preserved.

Ramo che i fortunali hanno sfrondato
è il mio; e i lacerti che vedi
sono i resti di lontane bufere.
Accelerai il tuo passo—Emily
della lombarda alta borghesia—
ed ora temo, per te, i dolori
che già furono i miei. In questo mondo
vuoto di speranza e dai confini incerti
pochi ti riconosceranno; anch'essi
consapevoli che d'ora in ora
si sta perdendo il centro
nel nostro tempo illume.

Mine is the branch the tempests
have unleaved; and the tattered hide you see
is what's survived from distant storms.
Your pace will quicken—Emily
of the Lombard upper-middle class—
and now I fear for you the pains
that once were mine. In this world
devoid of hope, with unsure boundaries,
few will recognize you; but they realize
as well that moment by moment
we're losing the center
in our lightless time.

SETTEMBRE

Le nubi si rincorrono nel cielo
giocando a rimpiattino, all'angolo
del viale, un piccolo gatto incappucciato
di nero, annusa l'aria intorno e
par che pensi—è l'ultima giornata
di vacanza. Finirà questo piacevole
ozio estivo, tornerò anch'io alla solita
poltrona. L'estate sta sfumando
tra nebbie di ricordi. Chissà
se avrò memoria degli ultimi barbagli
nel più velato sole cittadino.

Clouds chase each other in the sky
playing hide-and-seek, at the corner
of the avenue, a little cat hooded
in black sniffs the air and
seems to think—it's the last day
of vacation. This pleasing summer
otium will end, I too will return to my
usual armchair. Summer's evaporating
in mists of memories. Who knows
if I'll remember its last beams
under the dimmer city sun.

TEMPO DI DISTRUZIONE

Se fu follia a guidare la mano
degli eventi o desiderio d'autodistruzione
non ho capito mai.
In questo pot-pourri l'uomo confuse
i contorni delle cose. Smarrì
il fine e dubitò di tutto.
L'incertezza rimase a guidarne i passi.
Un giorno l'artefice del mirabile gioco
dirà: basta, il viaggio è terminato.
E intanto il tempo si sgrana nella desolata
realtà della vita, che è sempre stata amara.

Whether it was madness that guided the hand
of events or desire for self-destruction
I've never understood.
In this potpourri man mixed up
the shapes of things. He lost sight of his goal
and doubted everything.
Uncertainty remained to guide his steps.
One day the artificer of the marvelous
joke will say: enough, the journey's over.
And still time drains away in the desolate
reality of life, which has always been bitter.

Oggi un cinereo cielo grava
sulla città, rombi di tuoni coprono
lugubri fischi di sirene.
Anche il banchiere parla di crolli
in borsa, s'alternano i soliti corsi
è il simbolo della rincorsa.
Il meglio sfugge alla valutazione,
ma non può, non vuole saperlo l'uomo
che ritrova un volto, solo, nell'azione.
Non resta ormai che ripiegare
verso una solitaria inanità
per salvare la propria libera opinione.

Today an ashen sky
weighs on the city, groaning thunder
drowns out lugubrious sirens.
Even the banker talks about collapses
on the exchange, the same rates fluctuate,
symbol of the run-up.
The best escapes evaluation,
but the man who finds a face in action only
can't know it, doesn't want to.
All that's left now is to retreat
into a solitary vanity
to preserve one's free opinion.

È difficile vivere
senza fede alcuna;
ogni giorno una notizia
d'un massacro. E negli incastri
quotidiani, scorgiamo il cupo
segno del destino.
Anche le guglie sembrano
tetti bassi, ma una nota
un guizzo inaspettato
tra i rampicanti, o un ignoto
battitore che rilancia la palla
e la partita ricomincia.
È la battaglia della sopravvivenza.

It's hard to live
without some kind of faith;
every day there's news
of a massacre. And in our daily
ups and downs, we see the somber
sign of fate.
Even the spires
are like low roofs, but a note,
an unexpected flash
among the climbing vines, or an unknown
player serving the ball,
and the game begins again.
It's the battle for survival.

Qual è la differenza
tra la cicala e la formica,
tra il dissipatore e il parsimonioso,
se ambedue usciranno spogli
dal viaggio che alla fine
eguaglia? «*Non v'è né vinto
né vincitore*», il detto popolare
serve certo a indicare
la trappola mortale delle scelte.
Come barche vorremmo veleggiare
verso lidi migliori, ma restiamo
ancorati al nostro niente.

What's the difference
between the grasshopper and the ant,
the spendthrift and the miser,
if both return home naked
from the journey that leaves them
the same in the end? *"There's no winner
or loser,"* the old saw
evidently underlines
the mortal trap of choice.
Like boats we want to set sail
for better shores, but stay
anchored to our nothing.

Pioggia a Venezia, neve sopra i mille.
E qui, la nebbia filtra da tutte le fessure
si confonde col fumo della sigaretta. Se potesse
ovattare i miei ricordi, velarli, cancellare
il passato e lasciar solo un mozzicone
acceso, simbolo di ciò che resta.

Rain in Venice, snow at a thousand meters.
And here, the mist comes in through all the cracks
and blends with my cigarette smoke. If only it could
muffle my memories, veil them, erase
the past and leave only a lit
cigarette butt, symbol of what stays.

Un'intera produzione lillipuziana
è *the size of a book* del nostro
editore. Libri che s'intascano
facilmente, e al tempo stesso
possono essere ingoiati
da un elettroserpente di modeste
dimensioni. Ciò che il fanfano
dovrà evitare è di mutar in
pesce-volante, per poi cadere a
capofitto nella rete del male
nazionale: il provincial conformismo.
Cedendo alle tue istanze
perdono il pocket editore
di tutte le infrazioni
di percorso, ma il verdetto
è sospeso: avrà la maglia rosa?

"The size of a book"
of our publisher's whole list
is Lilliputian. Volumes that slip
easily into a pocket
and can also be swallowed
by a modest-sized vacuum
cleaner. What the scatterbrain
has to avoid is becoming
a flying-fish, and running headlong
into the net of our national
evil: provincial conformism.

Hearing your entreaties
I forgive the pocket publisher
all his infractions
along the way, but the verdict's
unsure: will he win the pink jersey?

Più storico che politico
non riuscirà certo a tenere
la nostra barca a galla, sono
troppe le falle a poppa e a prua.

Al di là di ogni inganno
politico-mondano, il mio augurio
oggi che s'intorbidano l'acque
è di non cangiare la sua dirittura.

More historian than man of politics
he certainly won't succeed
in keeping our ship afloat:
there are too many leaks at poop and prow.

Apart from every political-worldly
illusion, my wish today
now the waters are muddying
is that he maintain his course.

Siamo burattini mossi da mani ostili.
Non serve vedere le ingiustizie.
Tutto è ormai diruto. Si sfalda
anche il prodigio. Gli occhi sono stanchi.
L'ultimo tempo del vivere è vissuto.
Resta solo l'incantesimo d'un volo
da questa terra folgorata verso
un altro antro, nel quale affonderemo
per poi emergere con contorni sfumati.

We're puppets moved by hostile hands.
It doesn't help to see the injustices.
Everything's run down now. Even the miracle's
crumbling. Our eyes are tired.
The final time for living has been lived.
All that remains is the enchantment of a flight
from this thunderstruck earth to
another cave, into which we'll dive
to emerge later with vague outlines.

Si muove con Würde, libero
da falsi allettamenti,
alla prima lettura rivela
una musica che viene da lontano
e lo trascinerà verso quei lidi
dell'imaginare che è l'unico reale.
Nasce dalle stesse prode
che diedero i natali a un altro
geniale triestino. Auguro,
al tuo saggista prediletto,
di reggerne il confronto.
Al resto provvederà il destino.

He begins with Würde, free
of false enticements,
at first reading he reveals
a music that comes from afar
and will lead him toward those lands
of imagining, which is the sole reality.
He was born on the same shores
that gave life to another
genial Triestine. May your
favorite essayist
survive the comparison.
Destiny will see to the rest.

La solitudine di gruppo
ha da tempo trovato un rituale
nei Congressi a ripetizione.
Tutti abbozzano filosofie di vita,
inventano codici applicandoli a caso.
Le idee divengono merce di scambio.
Nella sala affollata da molti congressisti
forse nessuno ascolta l'altrui lezione.
Ripartiranno sazi e sorridenti
per ritrovarsi alla prossima «rencontre»
a riproporre altri sformati di nozioni.

Group solitude
has long since found a ritual
in recurring Conventions.
Everyone outlines philosophies of life,
invents systems and applies them randomly.
Ideas become media of exchange.
In the hall packed with conventioneers
it may be no one hears the other's talk.
They'll leave satisfied and smiling
to meet again at the next "rencontre"
and offer new idea-stews again.

IL RITRATTO

Come le note impetuose
s'arrestano, brillano nell'aria
e s'imprimono sul volto,
l'ansia che scivola sui tasti
e spande intorno un'ombra di dolore
vale più d'un ritratto.
Ti ricordo così, seduta al pianoforte
pronta a spiccare il volo.

The way the impetuous notes
halt, shine in the air
and get printed on your face,
the anxiousness that slithers on the keys
and radiates a shadow of unhappiness
is worth more than a portrait.
I remember you this way, sitting at the piano
ready to take flight.

Telefoni per ricordarmi
d'aver detto che il Nobel
dev'essere rifiutato, perché
non sempre è dato al migliore.
Forgive me, lo accetto per paura.
Un cospicuo compenso non offende
al contrario difende dalle insidie
della svalutazione. Non attenderti
gesti di coraggio da un vegliardo.
I riconoscimenti giungono
sempre in ritardo, quando sembra
inutile anche un titolo ambito.
Il tempo degli eventi
è diverso dal nostro.

You phone to remind me
I said the Nobel
ought to be refused, because
it's not always awarded to the best.
Forgive me, I'm accepting out of fear.
A conspicuous reward doesn't offend,
rather it's a defense against the threat
of devaluation. Don't expect
acts of courage from an old man.
Recognition always arrives
late, when even a hoped-for
honor seems useless.
The time of events
is different from ours.

Venne da me tutt'altro che sereno
di ritorno da una lunga seduta,
s'eran decise le sorti d'un poeta.
Disse d'aver covato serpi in seno
e di sentire un oscuro senso d'abiezione.
Era stanco, attorniato da nemici
prima striscianti ed ora pronti
a iniettar veleno.
—Sono un perdente senza redenzione.
L'amico, reo confesso,
aveva ritrovato la ragione.

He came to see me anything but serene
returning from a long session.
A poet's fate had been decided.
He said he'd harbored serpents in his breast
and felt a dark sort of dejectedness.
He was tired, ambushed by enemies,
fawning at first but ready now
to shoot their venom.
—I'm an unredeemed loser.
Having pled guilty, our friend
had recovered his reason.

Non lo sapremo mai, se furono
i passeri voraci a raccogliere
le briciole lasciate sul tavolo
del bar. Passò un motorscooter
e i tessitori celesti fuggirono
altrove a intrecciare volute.
In quel chiarore grigiorosa
del tramonto tardo estivo,
m'interrogai sul giorno ormai passato:
risposero, col loro canto,
i testimoni del nostro conversare.

We'll never know if it was the voracious
sparrows that snatched
the crumbs left on the café
table. A motorscooter passed
and the heavenly weavers flew
elsewhere to interlace their scrolls.
In the gray-pink brightness
of the late summer sunset,
I asked myself about the day now spent:
they answered, with their song,
witnesses to our conversation.

IL FILOLOGO

Con calze bianche e berretto di tela
ecco che giunge, in veste estiva,
il nostro maestro di filologia.
E se la luce tende a sfuocare
quel suo alone di mistero, egli
lo difende con lenti affumicate.
Così celato, sembra voler scrutare
il futuro ignoto a noi tutti.
I suoi gesti, esitanti, nascondono
paure, rivelano il timore
dell'oscuro male dell'universo.
Vorrei, per sottrarlo al silenzio, chiedergli
se il biondo tiziano dei tuoi riccioli
è da considerarsi un isabellismo
permanente o solo una variante;
ma un frullo d'ali m'interrompe.
L'amico ha captato il pensiero
sogguarda lungamente un lieve raggio
che si screzia sulla chioma lionata,
tamburellando enigmatico sul dorso
della mano con le dita; poi parla
del libro che curerete insieme.
Accenna a una seconda prefazione
delle nuove poesie, così risponde
mostrandomi ben altri tuoi valori.
Restiamo entrambi in ammirazione,
mentre il sole rinnova l'incanto
rigeneratore che ferma il tempo.

Sporting white socks and cloth beret
here he comes, in summer clothes,
our master of philology.
And if the light tends to lessen
his halo of mystery, he
protects it with his dark glasses.
Hidden this way, he seems to want to scrutinize
the future unknown to us all.
His gestures, hesistant, conceal
his fears, reveal his dread
of the dark ill of the universe.
To draw him out of his silence, I want
to ask him if the Titian blond of your curls
should be considered a permanent
isabellism or just a variant;
but a flutter of wings interrupts me.
Our friend has picked up on my thought,
he observes at length a ray of light
that's speckling your tawny mane,
enigmatically tapping his fingers
on the back of his hand; then he mentions
the book you'll edit together.
He refers to a second preface
to your new poems, his answer
instructing me in very different gifts of yours.
We're both lost in admiration,
while the sun renews the regenerative
magic that calls time to a halt.

ALL'AMICO *EDITOR*

Usciste insieme e udii
le vostre voci sino all'ascensore.
Poi, gli parlai del meglio
che viene tardi a galla,
dei bizzarri escamotages dei poeti.
Forte di ciò che lasciai trapelare,
cercherà di risolvere
l'enigma pluriennale.
E capirà che non fu solo un gioco,
ma si trattò di messaggi
inviati da un suggeritore imparziale.
Allora e solo allora,
scoprirà l'arcano d'una designazione,
e leggerà il cognome,
di chi sdegnava aiuti e compromessi,
nel motto che fiorisce sui frontespizi.

You exited together and I heard
your voices all the way to the elevator.
Afterwards, I spoke to him
of the best which surfaces late,
and poets' strange legerdemain.
Fortified with what I let drop,
he'll try to resolve
the now years-old conundrum.
And he'll know it wasn't just a game,
but a matter of messages
sent by an impartial prompter.
Then and only then
will he discover the meaning hidden in a sign
and read the name
of one who disdained help and compromise
in the motto that flowers on his title pages.

IL GINEVRINO

Scrittore e musico della parola
ha un percorso esemplare,
e lascia percettibili segnali
di quei filtri usati
per uomini e opere immortali.
Così, densi di pathos,
affiorano i ricordi dall'inconscio,
e la memoria in sé li affissa.
E si ripete il flusso
del nostro reversibile passato.

Writer and musician of the word
he's led an exemplary career,
and leaves perceptible signs
of the potions he has used
on immortal men and works.
So, dense with pathos,
recollections rise from the unconscious,
and memory saves them in itself.
And the flux of our reversible
past repeats itself.

La notte che s'insinua tra le pieghe
più oscure, ha capito l'arcano
del tempo, dello spazio che divide.
La verità è forse in questo lembo
che s'assottiglia, nel mozzicone spento,
riappare in quel fondo di bottiglia
abbandonato lungo la battigia.
Il resto, altro non è che un pretesto
per sentirsi vivi e meno soli.

The night that insinuates
in the deepest folds, has understood
the mystery of time, and space that separates.
Truth perhaps is in this vanishing
edge, this spent cigarette butt,
it reappears in that bottle bottom
left on the shoreline.
The rest is nothing but a pretext
for feeling alive and less alone.

Siccome ammiri la mia tendenza
a reagire con humour alle noie
quotidiane, confesso che da vecchi,
quando si tocca il fondo,
l'ironia è il solo modo
per non farsi sorprendere
col volto ingrigito dal dolore.
In tristitia hilaris, mi ripeto.
Sovente l'uomo inganna se stesso
è la perenne fuga dal presente:
unico schermo ai mali.

Since you admire my tendency
to respond to daily tedium
with humor, I confess that for the old,
once we hit bottom,
irony's the only way
not to be surprised
with a face gone gray with sadness.
In tristitia hilaris, I repeat.
Man often fools himself,
it's the perennial flight from the present:
the one shield against pain.

Resta lontano dalle secche
tu che cerchi il tutto
e rifiuti notorietà e fama.
Resta ancorata al bello, al sogno,
non cadere nell'inganno del presente.
L'amorosa musa t'aprirà le porte
dell'eliso e i suoni che distilli
ti compenseranno dell'amaro
sapore di critiche e silenzi.
I tuoi cristalli trasparenti
non periranno nella funerea scia,
già travalicano le lugubri scacchiere
che decidon le sorti.
Nell'ora cara agli dei
tutto muterà d'un tratto,
era già scritto.

Stay away from the sandbanks
you who seek after the all
and reject notoriety and fame.
Stay anchored to the beautiful, the dream,
don't fall into the illusion of the present.
The loving muse will open heaven's
gates for you, and the sounds that you distil
will repay you for the bitter taste
of criticism and silence.
Your transparent crystals
won't perish in the deathly wake,
already they're escaping the drab
chessboard that decides our fate.
In the hour dear to the gods
all will change in a flash,
it was already written.

In giorni come questi, spesso
la tetraggine m'assale
e il vivere d'ora in ora
mi tortura. Ma arrivi tu
che sconfiggi la noia
coi tuoi discorsi variopinti.
Anche oggi cercheremo una breccia.
Una parola nuova che ci possa salvare
e che ci tenga in bilico
sul confine ideale tra realtà
e fantasia potrà, anche
se per poco, cangiare l'esistenza.

In days like these,
gloom often assails me
and living from hour to hour
is torture. But then you come
who chase away boredom
with your parti-colored talk.
Today again we'll look for a way out.
A new word that will save us
and keep us poised
on the ideal edge between real
and imaginary can, even
if only briefly, change existence.

L'AMICA NAPOLETANA

Dopo un incontro in libreria
con l'amica dal crine fluente,
giungesti dicendo che coniugava
un calore nostrano con un esotismo
del tutto personale, la scrittrice napoletana
era una Yourcenar italiana.
E rinnovasti in me il ricordo
d'una femminista dalla voce di contralto,
una guerriera dagli occhi colmi
d'arcane voluttà.
Brandivi il suo romanzo,
e attendevi l'assenso
che non tardò, e la solarità
del volto ove dilagava la gioia
mi rivelò l'ultimo esemplare
d'una specie estinta.
Ti congedasti così, portatrice
d'un'invisibile bellezza.
Eri poeta e poesia, tu che con sguardo
virgineo spargevi fragranze intorno.
Il tuo sorriso, per me che t'ero amico,
fu il premio più ambito.

Having met your friend with the flowing
locks in a bookstore,
you arrived saying she combined
a warmth like ours with an exoticism
all her own: the Neapolitan
 writer was an Italian Yourcenar.
And you renewed a memory in me
of a feminist with a contralto's voice,
a warrior with eyes that overflowed
with secret sensualities.
You brandished her novel,
awaiting my assent
which wasn't slow, and the sunniness
of your face where joy was spreading
showed me the last exemplar
of an extinct species.
So you left me, bearer
of an invisible beauty.
You were poet and poetry, you whose virginal
look spread fragrances around you.
Your smile, for me your friend,
was the most coveted reward of all.

Il criterium era scontato
prima gli imitatori, i censori,
i detrattori e gli arrampicatori,
poi, ogni tanto, permettevano
che un dimenticato venisse pure a galla.
Il futuro della poesia è nelle mani
di uomini dal giudizio convenzionale.
Il poeta viene schedato
da sedicenti intenditori
che ignorano di essere sprovvisti
del giusto predicato.
Bravo, bravissimo scrivono
tutti in coro, ma chi sono costoro?
Speculatori di parole
o politici della penna
che esultano nell'omologare.
Ma poi svelano il gioco
del render tutto informe, tutti uguali.
E il turpe progetto porterà l'Italia
verso l'inevitabile sfascio totale.

The standard lost in value
first the imitators, censors,
the detractors and climbers,
then every so often they allowed
someone forgotten simply to float in.
The future of poetry is in the hands
of men with conventional taste.
The poet gets pegged
by so-called connoisseurs
who don't realize they lack
the necessary gift.
Bravo, bravissimo, they write
in unison, but who are they?
Word-speculators
or politicos of the pen
who revel in conformity.
But later they'll show their cards:
everything gone shapeless, every poetaster
just the same. And their base plan will carry Italy
to inevitable total disaster.

Tornerà la musica che assicura
la sopravvivenza della poesia,
e ne conserva la forma
propria della sua esistenza?
Scampati alle trappole mortali,
al groviglio dei suoni atonali,
s'avrà cura di tutte quelle note
che possono rompere il grigiore.
Volgano pure i pollici
i nuovi censori; ma il versificare,
da quando è caduto in loro balìa,
è da tempo ridotto all'agonia.

Will it return, the music that assures
the future life of poetry
and preserves the form
of its own being?
Having escaped the mortal traps,
the tangle of atonal sounds,
it will take care of all the notes
that can break the grayness.
Let the new censors
turn thumbs down; but making verse,
ever since it fell under their sway,
has long since been reduced to agony.

Può certo figurare nel Gotha
dei critici più illustri il visitor
che oggi è da me visiting.
Il giovane è cosciente
che non si fanno glosse
a una poesia inesistente.
E inoltre sa che compito del critico
è l'esplorare senza divenir criptico
per dare senso al niente.

He certainly belongs in the Almanach
de Gotha of the most distinguished critics,
the *visitor*
visiting me today. The young man knows
that one can't gloss
a nonexistent poem.
And he knows, too, that the critic's task
is to explore without becoming cryptic
in order to make sense of emptiness.

Sorta dall'isola che generò colombe
biancovestita giungi e ti porgo una fronda
a forma di ghirlanda.
Oh natura divina, animatrice di parole,
hai salvato l'anima mia dal naufragio
coi tuoi versi che sull'ali occulte
veleggeranno immortali, né premio
più bello poteva darmi la sorte.
Al domani chiederò un altro incontro
e un altro ancora, perché qui
di fronte, io vecchio vate e tu
giovane Saffo, siamo un oggi
non incenerito, né vuoto;
brilla nell'aria lo sfumato colore del prodigio.

Risen from the island that gave birth to doves
you arrive clad in white and I offer you a branch
in the form of a garland.
Oh divine nature, word animator,
you've saved my soul from drowning
with your lines which on occulted wings
will sail immortal, nor could fate
have granted me a lovelier reward.
Tomorrow I'll request another meeting
and another still, because here
face to face, I ancient bard and you
young Sappho, together we make up a now
that isn't ashes, or empty;
the pale color of the miracle gleams in the air.

Non so se preferisco
il giornalista o il brillante scrittore,
l'amico sincero o l'uomo d'onore.
Dicono sia un tennista
di valore, e so che è mal tollerato
dai colleghi, sia per il nome
che per la cultura o forse
per quel vezzo di portare
con *nonchalance* gli occhiali
sulla fronte. . . . . . l'elegante
giovin signore certo ha
una marcia in più.
Lo troverai simpaticamente
distaccato, qualità che noi ammiriamo,
e per la quale, dai più è detestato.

I don't know if I prefer
the journalist or the scintillating writer,
the sincere friend or the man of honor.
They say he's a talented
tennis player, and I know he's disliked
by his colleagues, because of his name
or his cultivation or maybe
for the vice of wearing
his glasses on his foreheard with such *nonchalance* . . .
the elegant young seigneur is surely
a step ahead.
You'll find him sympathetically
detached, a quality we admire
which means that he's detested by the crowd.

COLAZIONE ALL'AUGUSTUS

Tokaj e boccioli di salmone rosato,
melone e ogni leccornia,
nel ristorante all'aperto
con tendoni e sabbia tutt'intorno.
E al secondo rintocco attaccai
una romanza e poi un duetto.
La gente applaudì, la lancetta
del barometro segnava bonaccia.
Che sia l'effetto del vino
a rendermi così ottimista?
Una signora, d'un tavolo vicino,
dopo un mio trillo volle offrirmi
un fiore; forse per indicarmi
che una pausa poteva allietarla
più d'un dolcetonante acuto.

LUNCH AT THE AUGUSTUS

Tokay and pink salmon rosettes,
melon and all sorts of amuse-gueules,
in the outdoor restaurant
with awnings and sand all around.
And at the stroke of two I began
a romance and then a duet.
People applauded, the barometer
was indicating calm.
Was it the wine
that made me so optimistic?
A lady at the next table
offered me a flower
after my trill; maybe to suggest
a pause would be more pleasant
than a sweet-thundering baritone.

Fu allora che arrivasti
col caffetano bianco e udii
il crepitio dei passi sulla sabbia,
e come in un film muto,
gli occhi dei presenti
si volsero a guardare.
L'attore disse d'averti vista
lungo la battigia col caffetano
ed un turbante multicolore,
così in contrasto con le esibite
nudità estive. Sorridesti appena,
per la sua ammirazione,
ed era proprio quella sprezzatura
a renderti diversa: eburnea
e schiva. Non avevi bisogno
di sentirti lodare, tu bastavi
a te stessa. T'allontanasti lieve,
simile ad un gabbiano reale.
E da lontano vidi fondersi
l'argenteo zenit con il nitore
del bianco caffetano.

THE WHITE CAFTAN

It was then you arrived
with your white caftan and I heard
the crunch of your steps on the sand,
and as in a silent film,
the eyes of everyone present
turned to stare.
The actor said he'd seen you
along the water's edge in your caftan
and a multi-colored turban,
such contrast with the paraded
summer nudity. You barely smiled
at his admiration,
and it was just this nonchalance
that made you different: ivory white
and shy. You had no need
to hear praise, you were enough
for yourself. You walked on blithely,
like a royal gull.
And from afar I saw the silver
zenith meld with the brilliance
of your white caftan.

Porterai con te l'ultima ventata
di poesia; poi una nube gonfia
di presagi funesti oscurerà
la luce che ci fu concessa.
Non fosti un semplice bagliore,
giungesti inaspettata, voce di salvazione.
Un suono limpido emettono
i cristalli quando il vento
li sfiora, il chiarore li fa splendere
come incandescenti arcobaleni
che illuminano d'attorno.
Intorno il mondo scolora.

You'll bring with you the latest breeze
of poetry; then a swollen cloud
of deathly omens will obscure
the light that was granted to us.
You weren't a simple ray,
you came unexpected, voice of salvation.
Crystals emit
a clear sound when the wind
touches them, the brightness makes them shine
like incandescent rainbows
emanating light.
Around, the world goes colorless.

Ancora si crede che scrivere
poesia sia un fatto d'elezione.
Ed è di moda fare lo scrittore,
esserlo nell'aspetto, nella voce,
come se certe regole fossero
di rigore. Arrivano con
l'intrigo, senza salir le scale
usano l'ascensore.
Ma a che serve, se sono
sprovvisti di motore?
Vedo un tale vuoto;
è il trionfo del brutto,
degli stolti mascherati
da seri pensatori. Assisteremo
a lungo a questi orrori?

People still think writing
poetry is for the elect.
It's fashionable to play the writer,
to look and sound the part,
as if certain rules were
de rigueur. These arrive
by intrigue, they don't climb the stairs,
they take the elevator.
But what's the point,
if they don't have an engine?
I see such emptiness:
the triumph of the wrong,
of idiots disguised
as serious thinkers. How long
shall we be witness to these horrors?

Un alone che non vedi
ti circonda, figlia della luce.
Ti conduce verso altri lidi.
—Ha tutto—dice Gina—
ed è infelice—; certo non
può capire come soffre
chi sogna strade di cristallo,
calpestando ogni giorno
il nero asfalto.
Cuore d'altri non c'è
simile al tuo:
impetuoso e lieve.
Cerbiatta con gli umili
e leone coi potenti.
Sei motivo d'orgoglio
per chi vede in te
il germoglio che darà testimonianze.

A halo you don't see
surrounds you, daughter of light.
It leads you on to other shores.
Gina says, She has everything
yet she's unhappy; surely she can't
understand how one who dreams
of crystal streets
suffers treading the black
asphalt every day.
No other's heart
is like your heart:
impetuous and blithe.
Fawn with the timid
and lion with the strong.
You're a cause of pride
for him who sees in you
the seed that will bear witness.

Nell'orizzonte incerto d'una porta
l'indizio del tuo arrivo vibra nell'aria,
ma il pallore del tuo viso m'addolora
e il parlare è più stanco, mentre
racconti d'una lontana malattia,
e in quel tuo dire rifluisce il desiderio
d'oblio e di sparire sconosciuta.
Per anni anch'io camminai incerto,
poi mutò il vento, e risalii la china.
Oggi ti porgo un dono in forma di parole,
perché tu possa inerpicarti e resistere
alla sorte; hai già tre talismani:
penna, musica e colori.
Il tuo crederti inutile, che ripeti
sovente, mi fa dire: rimani, accetta,
anch'io sono un fallito come gli altri;
siamo dei condannati che cercano
una tregua e proprio mentre ogni cosa
sembrava incarbonirsi, quest'anime confuse
sentono accanto un'anima gemella.

In the uncertain horizon of a doorway
the sign of your arrival quivers in the air,
but the pallor of your face pains me
and your talk is more fatigued,
telling of a distant malady,
and back into your speech flows the desire
to be lost and disappear unknown.
For years I walked uncertain, too,
then the wind changed, and I climbed the slope again.
Today I offer you a gift in the form of words,
so you can scale the heights and resist
fate; you have three talismans already:
pen, music, paint.
The belief you're useless, which you often
mention, makes me say: Stay, accept,
I too am a failure like the others;
we're condemned men hoping
for a reprieve and just when everything
seemed to turn to charcoal, these confused souls
sense a twin spirit next to them.

Con gli occhi fissi
leggesti a voce bassa.
Tu scrivevi così, gareggiando
coi grandi, me n'accorsi
solo allora: tanto avara di te
sei sempre stata.
Dall'olimpo trai l'ingegno
ed io vo' darti un premio:
coronandoti fra l'Arti e le Muse,
perché la gente sappia
che l'invidioso riso
non li ornerà dell'eterno serto.

With steady eyes
you read in a low voice.
You wrote this way, vying
with the great, I saw it
only now: you've always been
so chary of yourself.
You bring your gift from Olympus
and I want to give you a prize:
to crown you among the Arts and Muses,
so the people will know
that envious laughter
won't win them the eternal wreath.

S'addensarono nuvole
e cirri minacciosi.
Un ombrellone cadde
e il vento turbinando
lo portò verso il mare.
T'alzasti, come una
paradisea reale
per salvarmi da un colpo
a sorpresa. Chiudesti
l'ombrellone che minacciava
il mio capo, con agili
mani da pianista.

Clouds gathered
and menacing fleece.
An umbrella fell
and the whirling wind
carried it toward the sea.
You rose, like a
royal bird of paradise
to save me from a sudden
blow. You closed
the umbrella that threatened
my head, with agile
pianist's hands.

Il tuo pallore
mi fece trasalire,
ti si leggeva in volto
quell'abbandono della vita.
E, come acqua limpida,
il tuo sguardo
disse il distacco
dalle umane cose, recavi
il tuo soffrire con te,
e rispondevi appena;
poi d'un tratto salutasti,
breve, e scivolasti via
lasciandomi col mio dolore, muto.

Your pallor
startled me,
I could read in your face
that abandonment of life.
And, like clear water,
your look
spoke of your detachment
from human things, you carried
your suffering with you,
and barely answered;
then suddenly you spoke to me
briefly, and slipped away
leaving me silent, with my pain.

Un'imbeccata e via
corre l'innocentino,
poi tra bisbigli divora
la sua preda
chiatton . . . chiattone
lungo la battigia.

A beakful and the innocent
thing runs off,
to devour his prey
whimpering
secretive
along the shore.

Nel giardino dei Giusti
c'erano il merlo e il pittore,
l'attore-regista e la maga.
In quel consesso, non
si poteva parlare, perché
tutti aspettavano la storica frase
del vate: attesi la filastrocca
del merlo, per poter celiare.
Tu ridevi per la comicità
della gaffe dell'ultima arrivata,
che volle divinare i segni.
Li elencò tutti ma non la bilancia.
La maga fu smagata.
Così, un imprevisto aveva mutato
il corso d'un'intera giornata.

In the garden of the Giusti
were the crow and the painter,
the actor-director and the witch.
In this assembly, no one
dared to say a word, for all
expected the bard's historic utterance:
I was waiting for the crow's
refrain, to make a joke.
You laughed at the comicality
of the gaffe of the last arrival,
who wanted to divine our signs.
She named every one but Libra.
The witch got ditched.
So something unexpected changed
the course of an entire day.

Nell'algida sera d'inverno
una folgore scosse le fronde
dell'albero, e una fiamma
avvampò. Ma si svelò,
subito, il mistero,
m'ero appisolato davanti
all'occhio nero del televisore.

In the frigid winter evening
lightning shook the trees'
leaves, and a flame
flared. But suddenly
the mystery was solved:
I'd dozed off in front
of the black eye of the television.

Il profumo dell'estate
era arrivato alle nari,
all'improvviso, dopo una grandinata.
Dura da anni questo passaggio
breve di stagioni; un quotidiano
ha sottolineato che da trent'anni
non si registrava un tale avvenimento,
statistica mancata,
i cronisti hanno la memoria corta.

The scent of summer
had reached the nostrils,
suddenly, after hail.
This brief change of seasons
has been happening for years; one daily noted
that a similar event
hasn't been observed for thirty years,
erroneous statistic;
reporters have short memories.

Quel giorno venne Angelica
l'istitutrice-educatrice,
che ti fece da madre.
La ricordo bruna e loquace,
ma nel suo brio svelava
un profondo sentire.
E ancor più mi colpì
quel suo grande amore
nell'inneggiare alla tua nobile figura.
Poi mutò registro
parlando di luoghi: Grado,
se ben ricordo. Mi piacque
quell'orgia di parole,
c'era qualcosa di prepotentemente
vivo in lei, una forza nativa.

That day Angelica
your tutor-teacher came,
who was like a mother to you.
I remember her brunette and talkative,
but in her brio she revealed
a deep sensitivity.
And even more, what struck me
was the great love with which
she hymned your noble profile.
Then she changed register
and talked of places: Grado,
if I recall correctly. I enjoyed
that orgy of words,
there was something overwhelmingly
alive in her, an innate power.

Un giorno non lontano
assisteremo alla collisione
dei pianeti e il diamantato cielo
finirà sommerso in avvalli.
Allora coglieremo rutilanti fiori
e stelle al neon.
Guarda, ecco il segnale, un fuoco
s'appicca in cielo, si scontrano
Giove con Orione e nel terribile
frastuono dov'è finito l'uomo?
Certo basta un soffio al mondo
in cui viviamo per scomparire.
Rimarrà forse un grido, quello
della terra che non vuole finire.

Someday not long from now
we'll watch the planets collide
and the diamond-studded sky
will end engulfed in craters.
Then we'll gather blazing flowers
and neon stars.
Look, the sign, a fire
peaks in the sky, Jupiter
crashes into Orion, and where has man
ended in the terrible uproar?
Certainly, in the world we live in
all it takes is a gust to disappear.
Maybe a single cry will survive,
that of the earth that doesn't want to end.

Deponete la vostra invidia.
Qui non c'è né un'oscura malia,
né il plauso ingiusto.
Spira in lei la stessa armonia
che è nei suoi versi.
Lasciate lo spirito perverso
e sentirete che è tornato il canto,
la musica dimenticata
d'un balzo ha ripreso il suo sentiero.

Pull down thy envy.
Here there's no evil spell,
or unjust applause.
The same harmony inhabits her
as lives in her lines.
Abandon your perverse spirit
and you will hear the song's returned,
the forgotten music
with one jump has recovered its groove.

Per scancellare il mio ricordo
basterà un giro d'altre voci,
è già troppo sperare d'essere
ricordato dagli amici.
L'uomo vive solo il presente,
alle donne è dato il ricordare.
Ma che importa, anche qui
l'unica verità che possiamo
constatare è di non sapere
se pensare e scrivere e parlare
significhi essere viventi.

All it will take to erase the memory of me
is a run of other voices,
it's already too much to hope
to be remembered by one's friends.
Man lives the present only,
remembering is for women.
But what does it matter, here too
the one truth we have proof of
is that we don't know if thinking
and writing and speaking
mean being alive.

Sentivo le ore insonni
pesare su me, come rocce oscure.
Nell'angusta stanza v'erano presenze strane:
fattucchiere, gnomi o fate
mi guardavano con occhi accesi.
Il silenzio ingigantiva luci ed ombre;
sbatté un vetro e i fantasmi ritrovarono
la via dell'aria, con guizzi estrosi:
erano lampi che solcavano le tenebre.
Solo, senza timore di chi
s'insinuò nel sonno a mia insaputa,
ritrovai le vie del sogno.

I felt the sleepless hours
weigh on me, like dark stones.
In the narrow room were strange presences:
wizards, gnomes, or fairies
watched me with burning eyes.
The silence made lights and shadows huge;
a window shook and the phantoms
found the airway, with fantastic gleamings:
they were flashes furrowing the shadows.
Alone, without fear of those
who infiltrated my sleep without my knowing,
I found the ways of the dream again.

Parlerai di me con lo stesso
fervore che t'accende quando
ricordi il nonno scomparso.
La morte non è il sonno,
è un lido dal quale non si torna;
lenta risuona e poi giunge,
è l'ora, e d'improvviso ti tocca
di sparire tra sassi e terra.

You'll speak of me with the same
fervor that ignites you when you
mention your dead grandfather.
Death isn't sleep,
it's a shore we don't return from;
its foot falls lightly, then it arrives,
the time has come, it's suddenly your turn
to vanish under rocks and dirt.

Vivremo mai nella nostra
comune di New York,
in un grattacielo al trentesimo piano,
con gli amici più cari?
L'inafferrabile e il re della baia,
il giudice-traduttore, il Sommo,
il serenissimo e il banchiere.
Il filologo, il saggista, il giornalista,
l'amica napoletana, il critico genovese,
il musico, Adelheit e l'editore,
Paola ed altri ancora.
Dall'alto potremo guardare
l'immenso parco, le siepi
fiorite d'azalee, i pruni
i mandorli, gli alberi bianchi-rosa.
Al sorger della luce veleggeremo
tra cuspidi e cristalli illuminati
della città ove risuonano sirene,
e lo sguardo spazierà lontano.
L'amicizia questo può:
donare oblio, e all'estremo
farci rivivere insieme in nuove albe.

Will we never live
in our commune in New York,
in a skyscraper on the thirtieth floor,
with our dearest friends?
The elusive one and the king of the bay,
the judge-translator, the Highest,
il Serenissimo and the banker.
The philologist, the essayist, the journalist,
the friend from Naples, the critic from Genoa,
the musician, Adelheit, the publisher,
Paola and others, too.
Up high we'll be able to see
the enormous park, the flowering
hedges of azalea, the plums,
the almonds, the white-pink trees.
When the light comes we'll sail
between spires and shining crystals
of the city where sirens sing,
and the eye will wander far.
Friendship can do this:
grant forgetfulness, and at the final hour
allow us to live again together in new dawns.

Difficile è credere
che sia un dono la vita,
quando si trascina una
stanca esistenza e il vivere
d'ora in ora ci tortura;
ma anche nei tuoi occhi
vedo brume di dolore.
Hanno già flagellato il tuo
giovane cuore? E rispose per te
il mare e un'ombra lieve
di cormorano. Tacevi
e sogguardavi mesta
l'orizzonte estremo.

It's hard to believe
life is a gift,
when we drag on a weary
existence and living
tortures us hour by hour;
but in your eyes, too,
I see mists of pain.
Have they already troubled your
young heart? The sea
and a tenuous cormorant's
shadow answered for you.
You were silent and sadly
eyed the final horizon.

Il creatore è al corrente
dello stridente passatempo
dei mortali, o la valutazione
di un giusto e di un criminale
può essere discrezionale?
Anche uno scrittore giubilato,
forse, se emette giudizi, può essere
giudicato per il terribile reato.

Is the creator au courant about
the strident sport of mortals,
or can there be discretion in
weighing a just man and a criminal?
Maybe a superannuated writer, too, can be
judged, if he makes judgments,
for his terrible felony.

The translator wishes to thank Nicola Gardini for his help
and advice in preparing this translation.
Dates are those written on the manuscripts.

SE LA MOSCA T'AVESSE VISTA . . . (1971) [p. 2]
 la mosca: La Mosca was the nickname of Montale's notably
  myopic longtime companion, Drusilla Tanzi (1885–1963),
  whom he married shortly before her death. See the "Xe-
  nia," written in her memory, in *Satura*.
 Gina: Gina Tiossi, Mosca's maid since 1944, who served as
  Montale's housekeeper and guardian in his last years, and
  who is a recurrent figure in his later poetry.

20 GENNAIO O 30 ANNI (1971) [p. 4]
 20 gennaio: Birthday of Annalisa Cima.
 una musa: Erato, muse of lyric and love poetry.
 Emily: Emily Dickinson. Montale's translation of one of her
  poems appears in his *Quaderno di traduzioni*. Several of
  the Montale/Cima versions of Dickinson can be found in
  the Mondadori Meridiani edition of her work, edited by
  Marisa Bulgheroni.

QUANDO SARAI IMPERATRICE . . . (1973) [p. 6]
 The first line alludes to Annalisa Cima's "Habsburg" Aus-
  trian background.
 due amici: The poet and the critic Cesare Segre, who appears
  elsewhere in the Diary (see "Il filologo").
 ma nulla torna. . . : Angelini (198), referring to Paolo De Caro
  (see bibliography): "To us on earth, from the world of the
  dead, the beyond and memory."

AGILE MESSAGGERO ECCOTI (1973) [p. 8]
 Adelheit: The young Adelaide Bellinguardi worked in Rome
  as a public relations officer for the jeweller Bulgari. She ap-

pears as Chantal in "Il trionfo della spazzatura" and in "Diamantina" as Adelheit in *Diario del '71 e del '72*.

Agrodolce: Typical neo-stilnovistic epithet for Annalisa Cima.

È SOLO UN VIZIO (1973) [p. 10]

EX ABRUPTO (1975) [p. 12]
    e limpido risuona un verso: See Annalisa Cima's poem "Terso profilo di mare," dedicated to Montale, in her *Ipotesi d'amore* (1984).
    estintore: Literally, fire extinguisher; figuratively, successor.

MATTINATA (1969) [p. 14]
    The poem is rich in echoes of Montale's early work.
    col girasole: Cf. "Portami il girasole" in *Ossi di seppia*.
    Ad ogni apparizione . . . : Cf. "Crisalide" in *Ossi di seppia*: "Ogni attimo vi porta nuove fronde" ("Every moment brings new leaves to you").

LA FOCE (1969) [p. 16]
    "La foce" was the original title of "Incontro" in *Ossi di seppia*. Its setting is the point in Genoa where the river Bisagno meets the sea; the poem makes it clear, however, that the encounter is primarily a metaphorical one, of life and death: "ma più foce di umani atti consunti, / d'impallidite vite tramontanti / oltre il confine . . ." ("but more a mouth of withered human acts, / of wan lives setting over the horizon . . .").
    i vecchi rami: The Dantesque metaphor of man as a tree, developed in the wood of suicides in *Inferno* XIII, is found throughout Montale. See, for example, "Arsenio" in *Ossi di seppia* and "Personae separatae" in *La bufera e altro*.
    nell'attesa: Cf. the osso breve "Gloria del disteso mezzogiorno" in *Ossi di seppia*: "ma in attendere è gioia più compita" ("but there's greater joy in waiting").

MA C'È CHI (1973) [p. 18]
    Potius mori quam foedari: "Better to die than be contaminated." Motto attributed to Cardinal Jacobo of Lusitania, also known as Giacomo di Portogallo, archbishop of Lis-

bon and nephew of King Alfonso of Portugal (he died in 1459, aged 26), "a model of neo-Platonic purity," according to Angelini (199). The saying is referred to on his tomb, sculpted by Antonio Rossellino, in the church of San Miniato al Monte outside Florence (De Caro 152, q.v. for a complex investigation of Montale's potential sources for this poem).

IL CLOU (1977) [p. 20]

Ratio ultima rerum . . . id est deus. Leibniz (*Monadology* ¶38): "The ultimate reason for things . . . that is God."

nulla torna: See the same figure of speech in "Quando sarai imperatrice."

DIE FLEDERMAUS (1977) [p. 22]

uno smarrito adolescente: Montale's description of his young self in "Riviere," in *Ossi di seppia.*

aureola di cerchietti/fumiganti: The "smoky" halo of Annalisa Cima's curls recalls the spiraling cigarette smoke in "Nuove stanze" in *Le occasioni,* a sign of Clizia's sphinx-like presence.

il pipistrello: The operetta in question is Johann Straus II's *Die Fledermaus* (1874).

As a young man, Montale studied to be an opera singer, and he remained avidly interested in lyric drama all his life. In the 1950s and '60s, as the music critic for Milan's *Corriere della Sera,* widely considered the Italian paper of record, he reviewed many performances at La Scala and elsewhere (see his music criticism, collected in *Prime alla Scala,* Mondadori, 1981, and now in *Il secondo mestiere: Arte, musica, società*).

L'INAFFERABILE TUA AMICA SCRIVE (1977) [p. 24]

La critica: The literary critic Marisa Bulgheroni. The poem turns on the poet's punning parsing of her given name.

del ben noto Milanese: According to De Caro (145–146), Stendhal—whose chosen epitaph was *"Qui giace Arrigo Beyle Milanese; visse, scrisse amò"* [Here lies Henri Beyle, Milanese; he lived, he wrote, he loved], and who, in the first chapter of his *Vie de Rossini* describes how the aria "Di tanti

173

palpiti" from *Tancredi*, also known as "l'aria dei rizi," was written in the few minutes it took Rossini's cook to prepare the rice for his risotto).

con sottofondo di corno-inglese: Montale is referring to Bulgheroni's essay about Montale's translation of Emily Dickinson's poem, "There came a wind like a bugle," which her first editors called "The Storm," and its relation to Montale's early poem "Corno inglese." (See "Dickinson/Montale: Il passo sull'erba" in *Eugenio Montale: Profilo di un autore*, ed. Annalisa Cima and Cesare Segre [Rizzoli, 1977], 91–114).

MORTALI (1970) [p. 26]

LA CONGETTURA CHE IL MONDO (1970) [p. 28]
Cf. the final chorus of Verdi's *Falstaff*:

Tutto nel mondo è burla.
L'uomo è nato burlone,
La fede in cor gli ciurla,
Gli ciurla la ragione.
Tutti gabbati! Irride
L'un l'altro ogni mortal.
Ma ride ben chi ride
La risata final.

[All in the world's a hoax. / Man's born a huckster, / Faith wavers in his heart, / As reason vacillates. / Everyone's swindled! Every / Mortal mocks every other. / But he laughs well who laughs / The last laugh.]

ED ECCO, NEL TENTATIVO MALDESTRO (1970) [p. 30]
sulle spiagge stranote del banale: Cf. "i limiti del 'Brutto'" [tr.] in "Contrabasso," section 3 of the early "Accordi," in *Altri versi.*
un eone decaduto: neo-Platonic, gnostic terminology.

AL FORTE (1972) [p. 32]
Forte dei Marmi, a fashionable Tuscan beachside resort where Montale habitually spent the summer, beginning in 1946.

Paola: Paola Brovedani, a friend of Annalisa Cima's whom Montale once met at Forte dei Marmi.

NEL GIARDINO (1976) [p. 34]
Marchese (316): "The epiphany of the woman, the central theme of Montale's poetry, occurs in a scenario at once realistic and symbolic. Her consubstantiality with heaven is underlined by the verbs ("discendi," "sovrasta"), which exalt the figure of the woman angel come down from on high and crowned with azure . . . The apparent humility of the event reveals a religious outrage, the miracle of the woman who defeats the banal repetitiveness of time."
Nervi: Birthplace of Montale's mother Giuseppina Ricci, near Genoa.

RICORDO (1976) [p. 36]
Lei solo percepiva i suoni: The subject is Montale's wife, Drusilla Tanzi.

IN THE YEAR 2000 (1972) [p. 38]

OGGI È DI MODA (1972) [p. 40]

INCONTRO (1976) [p. 42]

SECONDO TESTAMENTO (1976) [p. 44]
The title evokes "Piccolo testamento," one of the two "Conclusioni provvisorie," or "Provisional Conclusions," at the end of *La bufera e altro*, which in turn refers to the testaments of François Villon.
del prima e dell'ignoto: Angelini (202): "Possible interpretations: first 'the horror' or the 'mal di vivere,' later the leap into the beyond; or rather: what I seemed to be, and what later will be known about me (my true face, unknown before); or again: this poem written in my old age will avenge me and itself for what I wrote previously and has remained unknown or misunderstood, because not comprehended in all its metaphysical and apocalyptic dimensions."
nel suo inganno di sempre: Cf. "l'inganno consueto," "the usual deceit," of the *osso* "Forse un mattino andando in un aria di vetro," in *Ossi di seppia*.

la bottiglia: Cf. "Su una lettera non scritta" in *La bufera*, where Montale evokes Alfred de Vigny's "bouteille à la mer" to represent the poet's tempest-tossed, solitary message to the beloved and, by extension, his reader.

L'AMICO LIGURE (1976) [p. 46]
The friend is the writer Vico Faggi (pseudonym of the Genoese judge, dramatist, and translator from Latin Alessandro Orengo).
Fagacee: Fagaceae: A family of deciduous trees and shrubs that includes the Fagus (beech—*faggio* in Italian), Castanea (chestnut), and Quercus (oak).
un libro di traduzioni: Faggi's translation of Seneca's *Oedipus*, which had recently been published by Einaudi.

COME MADRE (1976) [p. 48]
Monte Amiata: The largest mountain in Southern Tuscany and a significant locale in Montale's poetry (see "Notizie dall'Amiata" in *Le occasioni*).
la folata: Marchese (319): "The wind in Montale's poetry is often a sign of life or at least of the hope for an imminent existential renewal." Cf. the first line of "Vento e bandiere" in *Ossi di seppia*: "Il vento che alzò l'amaro aroma."
viviamo come trote . . .: Cf. "Vasca" in *Ossi di seppia*. The Orphic image of something emerging out of the chthonic depths of a well or pool goes back to the *osso breve* "Cigola la carrucola del pozzo," while the trout enshrouded in mud evokes themes in "L'anguilla" in *La bufera*. But "while 'L'anguilla' turns on the comparison of fish and woman (both of which tend to perpetuate life), here it is the poet who projects himself into the trout's reproductive instinct, to feel 'like a mother,' 'a womb for those who won't forget me'" (Marchese, 320).
alvo: literally, womb. Montale is conceiving himself here as Cima's poetic parent (as in the first poem in the diary).

LA FELICITÀ (1969 or 1970) [p. 50]
Resta nel tuo eliso: Cf. the command in "Incantesimo" in *La bufera*, where the poet commands his ephebe/lover, "Oh

resta chiusa e libera / nell'isole del tuo pensiero e del mio"
("Oh stay locked and free / in the islands of your thought
and mine").

Ben altro / è la felicità: Cf. "Elegia di Pico Farnese" in *Le oc-
casioni*: "Ben altro è l'Amore" ("Love is something else").

L'INSONNIA (1970)   [p. 52]
Montale was a lifelong insomniac and imagery of sleep-
lessness can be found elsewhere in his work, e.g. in "Giorno e
notte" in *La bufera e altro*.

L'ESTATE È SCOSSA DA FORTI TEMPORALI. (1970)
[p. 54]
The storm is a dominant image—and metaphor—throughout
Montale, particularly in *La bufera e altro*, where it assumes
apocalyptic dimensions. Here, as elsewhere in the last poems,
however, it has receded to purely nominal status.
una petroliera: Cf. "La casa dei doganieri" in *Le occasioni*.

HONORIS CAUSA (1970)   [p. 56]
The poem turns on the multiple meanings of the word *laurea*,
which denotes both an advanced academic degree and the
laurea honoris causa, or honorary degree, while also evoking
the classic poet's laurel crown. Angelini (203) tells us that
Montale himself received five honorary degrees, from the uni-
versities of Milan (1961), Cambridge (1967), Rome and Basel
(1974), and Nice (1976). The ironic treatment of the theme re-
calls Montale's rejection of the "poeti laureati" in his early *ars
poetica*, "I limoni," in *Ossi di seppia*.

INCERTEZZE (1970)   [p. 58]

L'INVESTITURA (1974)   [p. 60]
il Serenissimo: The poet Andrea Zanzotto was born in Pieve
di Soligo (Treviso) in the Veneto in 1921 and lived in Venice,
known as *la Serenissima*, the most serene of cities). His
book, *La beltà* [Beauty], was published by Mondadori in
1968 and Montale wrote an influential review of it (*Corriere
della sera*, 1 June 1968; in E.M., *Il secondo mestiere: Prose
1920–1979*, vol. 2, 2891–2895).

dopo una fumata: After a smoke, but also an allusion to the smoke puffs that signal the election of a new pope.

hochetus: A grieving duet sung during a funeral, a polyphonic composition characterized by a continuous breaking of the voices (from the French *hoquet*, or sob).

KING OF THE BAY (1970) [p. 62]

caput mundi: Head or top of the world.

Marianne, Djuna: Marianne Moore and Djuna Barnes, both at the time residents of New York City.

il re della baia: Luciano Rebay, professor of Italian literature at Columbia University, friend of the poet and author of incisive critical articles about his work.

L'ESEGETA (1972) [p. 64]

Fourier: The French social critic F. M. C. Fourier (1772–1837) recommended the organization of society into small communes (phalansteries).

Il Sommo: Nickname for Montale's oldest friend, the poet and critic Sergio Solmi (1899–1981), whom Montale met in military training at Parma in 1917.

A SUFFICIENZA NE ABBIAMO DI UN MONDO (1972) [p. 66]

RAMO CHE I FORTUNALI HANNO SFRONDATO (1974) [p. 68]

Written in response to a poem in Annalisa Cima's *Immobilità* (Scheiwiller, 1974), which begins:

Hai occhi nei rami sospesi
e dove i rami finiscono
hai radici profonde.

[You have eyes hanging in the branches / and where the branches end / you have deep roots.]

Cf. also Montale's December 1926 letter to Italo Svevo (Italo Svevo-Eugenio Montale, *Carteggio, con gli scritti di Montale su Svevo*, ed. Giorgio Zampa. Milan: Arnoldo Mondadori Editore, 1976, 39–40): "I am a tree that has long been burned by the *scirocco*, and everything I could give in the way of stifled cries is all in *Ossi di seppia* . . ." De Caro (203) notes an affinity with the first lines of Shakespeare's Sonnet 73 (from which Montale drew the epigraph for Part IV of *Le occasioni*).

SETTEMBRE (1974) [p. 70]

TEMPO DI DISTRUZIONE (1976) [p. 72]
il tempo si sgrana: The image goes back to "Vento e bandiere" in *Ossi di seppia*; cf. also the unbeading necklace in "Dal treno" in *La bufera*.

OGGI UN CINEREO CIELO GRAVA (1969) [p. 74]
the banker: Raffaele Mattioli, Milanese banker and noted patron of the arts.
un volto: Cf. the action of finding a face, or discovering or forming a character for oneself, in *Ossi di seppia*, e.g. in "Portovenere" and "Incontro."

È DIFFICILE VIVERE (1970) [p. 76]
Written on the gray tissue lining of an envelope.
un guizzo inaspettato / tra i rampicanti: The light flash, Montale's most frequent image—of presence, of inspiration, love, or life itself. Here, the setting recalls the "lit ivy" in "Fiesta fiesolana" in *La bufera e altro*.

QUAL È LA DIFFERENZA (1970) [p. 78]

PIOGGIA A VENEZIA, NEVE SOPRA I MILLE. (1970) [p. 80]
un mozzicone / acceso: An ironic reprise of the "favilla d'un tirso" at the end of "Mediterraneo" (in *Ossi di seppia*).

IL PESCE PILOTA (1973) [p. 82]
del nostro editore: Vanni Schweiwiller (1934–1999), publisher, like his father Giovanni, of a distinguished line of books, many of them of small dimensions, issued under the imprint All'Insegna del Pesce d'Oro (At the Sign of the Golden Fish; hence the title).
fanfano: Venetian dialect for the "pesce-pilota;" idiomatically speaking, a scatterbrain.
Cedendo . . . : Annalisa Cima writes: "[Montale] accedes to

my request and forgives Vanni for having published his
poems in several 'plaquettes' with drawings and paintings
by painters Montale did not like. The pink jersey is an allu-
sion to the fact that Vanni carried his little books around on
his bicycle and the pink [or yellow] jersey goes to the win-
ner of bicycle races."

ALL'ONOREVOLE-DIRETTORE (1976)   [p. 84]
Giovanni Spadolini (1925–1994), was a noted Italian political
historian, professor of law, director of *Il Corriere della Sera*; a
member of the Republican Party, he entered the Italian Sen-
ate in 1972. He served as Prime Minister of Italy (1981–1982)
and later as President of the Senate.
la nostra barca: The ship of state; the metaphor goes back to
Horace, *Odes* I, 14.

SIAMO BURATTINI MOSSI DA MANI OSTILI. (1970)
[p. 86]
The poem is rich in allusions to classic Montalean tropes:
Tutto è ormai diruto: Cf. "Flussi" in *Ossi di seppia*: "se pur
tutto è diruto" ("though everything's / run down").
questa terra folgorata: A quotation from "L'arca," in *La
bufera*.
un altr'antro: Cf. the caves in "Nubi color magenta" and in
"Da un lago svizzero"—a Platonic locus to which the poet
and his lover flee.
per poi emergere: Cf. "Giorno e notte" in *La bufera e altro*:
"questa dura / fatica di affondare per risorgere eguali"
("and always / this painful effort to sink under / to re-
emerge the same").

IL SAGGISTA PREDILETTO (1975)   [p. 88]
The critic and novelist Claudio Magris (born in Trieste, 1939),
author of *Danubio* and other noted works.
Würde: German for dignity.
una musica che viene da lontano: Allusion to Magris's book,
*Lontano da dove: Joseph Roth e la tradizione ebraico-
orientale*, Einaudi, 1971.

e lo trascinerà verso quei lidi: Cf. "I morti" in *Ossi di seppia*: "li volge fino a queste spiagge" ("drives them to these beaches").

un altro geniale triestino: the novelist Italo Svevo, whose Italian reputation Montale was instrumental in establishing. See "Italo Svevo in the Centenary of His Birth" in *The Second Life of Art: Selected Essays of Eugenio Montale*, 92–117.

LA SOLITUDINE DI GRUPPO (1975) [p. 90]
Cf. other poems on this theme, including "Al congresso" (1971) in *Diario del '71 e del '72* and "Siamo alla solitudine del gruppo" (1975) in *Quaderno di quattro anni*.

IL RITRATTO (1975) [p. 92]
Cf. the "osso" "Tentava la vostra mano la tastiera" in *Ossi di seppia*, which also portrays a pianist at the keyboard.

TELEFONI PER RICORDARMI (1975) [p. 94]
Montale learned that he had been awarded the Nobel Prize in Literature on October 23, 1975.

VENNE DA ME TUTT'ALTRO CHE SERENO (1974?) [p. 96]
sereno: The poet Vittorio Sereni (1913–1983) was then the poetry editor at Mondadori.

NO LO SAPREMO MAI, SE FURONO (1975) [p. 98]
This text too is rich in ironic echoes of Montale's early work:
Non la sapremo mai: Cf. the *osso breve* "Noi non sappiamo quale sortiremo" ("We don't know how we'll turn up").
i passeri: Leopardi's "passero solitario" is mentioned in "Annetta" in *Diario del '71 e del '72* and "I nascondigli II" in *Altri versi*. For a discussion of the significance of bird imagery in Montale, see the notes to "Il gallo cedrone" in *Collected Poems 1920–1954*, especially 590–591.
grigiorosa: Cf. "grigiorosea," an early Montalean adjective, borrowed from Montale's immediate precursors, the Ligurian *crepuscolari*, or twilight poets: it occurs in the early poem "Falsetto" in *Ossi di seppia*.

i tessitori celesti: In the last lines of "Tempi di Bellosguardo" in *Le occasioni*, the (feminine) "heavenly weavers" are locusts.

IL FILOLOGO (1975)   [p. 100]

The subject is the critic Cesare Segre (born 1928), professor of Romance Philology at the University of Pavia.

dell'oscuro male dell'universo: Cf. "dall'oscuro male uni-
· verso," the originary wound striking both the poet and his first beloved, in the early uncollected poem "Lettera levantina" (in *Altri versi*).

un isabellismo: "Isabella" is the Italian term for the tawny or reddish color also found in the plumage of certain birds.

il libro che curerete insieme: Eugenio Montale: Profilo di un autore, ed. Annalisa Cima and Cesare Segre (Rizzoli, 1977).

una seconda prefazione: to Cima's book *Sesamon* (Ugo Guanda Editore, 1977); the first was to her *Immobilità* (Schewiller, 1974).

ALL'AMICO EDITOR (1975)   [p. 102]

Marco Forti, Montale's publisher at Mondadori and the author of critical works on him.

nel motto: The famous Mondadori poetry collection, named after the review *Lo specchio*, carried the Dantesque motto "In Su La Cima" (at the summit) (*Paradiso* XIII, 135) on its title pages.

IL GINEVRINO (1976)   [p. 104]

The literary critic Jean Starobinski (born in Geneva in 1920), professor of literature at the University of Geneva, a "musician of the word" "capable of raising us, with his hermeneutic art that conjoins style and psychology, to the level of 'immortal men and works'" (Marchese).

e la memoria in sé li affissa: Cf. "Vecchi versi" in *Le occasioni*, "e la memoria / in sé le cresce" ("and they're magnified in memory").

LA NOTTE CHE S'INSINUA TRA LE PIEGHE (1976)
[p. 106]

SICCOME AMMIRI LA MIA TENDENZA (1976) [p. 108]
  In tristitia hilaris: Celebrated motto of the philosopher Giordano Bruno (1548–1600): *In tristitia hilaris, in hilaritate tristis* (Happy in sadness, sad in happiness).

RESTA LONTANO DALLE SECCHE (1974) [p. 110]
  Resta: Compare the opening of "Incantesimo" in *La bufera e altro*: "O resta chiusa e libera nell'isole / del tuo pensiero e del mio," ("Oh stay locked and free / in the islands of your thought and mine").
  L'amorosa musa: Again, Erato, muse of love poetry.
  le lugubre scacchiere: Annalisa Cima writes: "they leave behind the sad selections of the critics (allusion to anthologies)."

IN GIORNI COME QUESTI, SPESSO (1974) [p. 112]

L'AMICA NAPOLETANA (1974) [p. 114]
  The Neapolitan poet and writer Armanda Guiducci (1923–1994), author of *La domenica della rivoluzione* (1961); *Poesie per un uomo* (1965); *La mela e il serpente* (1974) (the book referred to in the poem); *Due donne da buttare* (1976); etc.

IL CRITERIUM ERA SCONTATO (1974) [p. 116]

TORNERÀ LA MUSICA CHE ASSICURA (1976) [p. 118]

AL GIOVANE CRITICO GENOVESE (1976) [p. 120]
  Angelo Marchese (1937–2000), whose book *Visiting angel: Interpretazione semiologica della poesia di Montale* (Turin: SEI, 1977) was highly regarded by Montale.

SORTA DALL'ISOLA CHE GENERÒ COLOMBE (1971)
  [p. 122]
  island: Willed confusion of the islands of Cyprus, mythic home of the dove, and Capri, where Annalisa Cima had been staying.

NON SO SE PREFERISCO [p. 124]
  The poem's subject is the journalist Gaspare Barbiellini Amidei, vice-director of *Il Corriere della Sera* from 1974 to 1987.

COLAZIONE ALL'AUGUSTUS (1975) [p. 126]
The scene is a restaurant in Forte dei Marmi.

IL CAFFETANO BIANCO (1976) [p. 128]
L'attore: Carmelo Bene.

PORTERAI CON TE L'ULTIMA VENTATA (1976) [p. 130]
Intorno il mondo scolora: The poem echoes "Incantesimo" in
La bufera e altro: "Intorno il mondo stinge" ("The world
around fades out").

ANCORA SI CREDE CHE SCRIVERE (1977) [p. 132]

UN ALONE CHE NON VEDI (1969) [p. 134]
figlia della luce: Recalls the Hölderlin-inspired Neoplatonic
poems for Volpe in *La bufera e altro*, e.g., "Per un 'Omag-
gio a Rimbaud,'" where Volpe is referred to as "figlia del
sole" ("daughter of the sun").
Cuore d'altri. . . . : Cf. "Iride" in *La bufera*: "Cuore d'altri
non è simile al tuo, / la lince non somiglia al bel soriano /
che apposta l'uccello mosca sull'alloro" ("Another's heart
is not your heart, / the lynx is nothing like the lovely
tabby, / stalking the hummingbird up in the laurel").

NELL'ORIZZONTE INCERTO D'UNA PORTA (1979)
[p. 136]
We find echoes of numerous poems here:
poi mutò il vento: cf. "Accelerato" in *Le occasioni* ("poi . . .
mutò il vento" ["then came . . . another wind"]).
Oggi ti porgo un dono: "Casa sul mare" in *Ossi di seppia*: "Ti
dono anche l'avara mia speranza" ("And I'm leaving you
my miser's hope").
mentre ogni cosa / sembrava incarbonirsi: "L'anguilla" in *La
bufera e altro*: "quando tutto pare / incarbonirsi" ("when
everything seems charcoal").

CON GLI OCCHI FISSI (1970) [p. 138]

S'ADDENSARONO NUVOLE (1972) [p. 140]

IL TUO PALLORE (1973) [p. 142]
recavi / il tuo soffrire con te: Cf. the *osso breve* "Ripenso il tuo
sorriso . . ." in *Ossi di seppia*: "o vero tu sei dei raminghi che

il male del mondo estenua / e recano il loro soffrire con sé come un talismano" ("or if you're one of those wanderers the world's evil harms / who carry their suffering with them like a charm").

poi d'un tratto salutasti: Cf. the last lines of "La bufera" in *La bufera e altro*: "Come quando / ti rivolgesti e con la mano. . . . / mi salutasti—per entrar nel buio" (As when / you turned and . . . waved to me—and went into the dark").

lasciandomi col mio dolore, muto: Cf. "Ballata scritta in una clinica" in *La bufera e altro*; "e pol l'ululo / del cane di legno è il mio, muto" ("and the bulldog's howl, unuttered, is my own").

UN'IMBECCATA E VIA (1974)   [p. 144]

NEL GIARDINO DEI GIUSTI (1975)   [p. 146]
Written on a postcard. The poem is set in the garden of Susi and Antonio Giusti, often Montale's hosts at Forte dei Marmi.
Characters: *The painter*: Nino Tirrinanzi; *the actor-director*: Carmelo Bene; *the witch*: Lucia Alberti, a visitor from Rome who attempted to guess the signs of those present, but misjudged Montale's, which is Libra.

NELL'ALGIDA SERA D'INVERNO (1975)   [p. 148]

IL PROFUMO DELL'ESTATE (1976)   [p. 150]
Written on a postcard from Forte dei Marmi. The reference to an erroneous newspaper report of a natural occurrence echoes the Volpean lyric "Dal treno" in *La bufera altro*.

QUEL GIORNO VENNE ANGELICA (1976)   [p. 152]
Annalisa Cima's nurse, Angelica Ruggero Calderoldi, a native of the Veneto, talked with Montale about Grado, on the Adriatic coast not far from Trieste.

UN GIORNO NON LONTANO (1977)   [p. 154]

DEPONETE LA VOSTRA INVIDIA (1977)   [p. 156]
Deponete . . . : Allusion to Pound's great passage "Pull down thy vanity" at the end of Canto LXXXI in the *Pisan Cantos*.

d'un balzo ha ripreso il suo sentiero: The image of the record skipping and then recovering its groove can be found in "Sotto la pioggia" in *Le occasioni*; see also in "L'orto" in *La bufera e altro*.

PER SCANCELLARE IL MIO RICORDO (1978)   [p. 158]
Postcard from Forte dei Marmi (1978).

Montale's fear of being supplanted, of eventual oblivion for his work, goes all the way back to "Potessi almeno costringere" in *Mediterraneo* in *Ossi di seppia*: "non ho che queste frasi stancate / che portranno rubarmi anche domani / gli studenti canaglie in versi veri" ("only these tired-out phrases / the student rabble can steal tomorrow / to make real poetry").

SENTIVO LE ORE INSONNE (August 1979)   [p. 160]
The setting, imagery and language here recall the intrusive insect of "Vecchi versi" in *Le occasioni*.

PARLERAI DI ME CON LO STESSO (1979)   [p. 162]

VIVEREMO MAI NELLA NOSTRA (1977)   [p. 164]
Another *plazer*, a typical poem of the *dolce stil nuovo* which expresses a fantastical, unrealizable wish, in this case the gathering-together of a commune or phalanstery composed of the poet, Cima, and all their friends who appear in the *Diario*: *l'inafferabile*: Marisa Bulgheroni; *il re della baia*: Luciano Rebay; *il giudice-traduttore*: Vico Faggi; *il Sommo*: Sergio Solmi; *il serenissimo*: Andrea Zanzotto; *il banchiere*: Raffaele Mattioli; *il filologo*: Cesare Segre; *il saggista*: Claudio Magris; *il giornalista*: Gaspare Barbiellini Amidei; *l'amica napoletana*: Armanda Guiducci; *il critico genovese*: Angelo Marchese; *il musico*: Jean Starobinski; *Adelheit*: Adelheit Bellinguardi; *l'editore*: Vanni Scheiwiller; *Paola*: Paola Brovedani.

DIFFICILE È CREDERE (undated)   [p. 166]
un'ombra lieve / di cormorano: Cf. "Incontro" at the end of *Ossi di seppia*: "alta si flette un'ala / di cormorano."

IL CREATORE È AL CORRENTE   [p. 168]
undated postcard from Forte dei Marmi.

SELECT BIBLIOGRAPHY

WORKS OF EUGENIO MONTALE

Diario postumo: prima parte: 30 poesie. Ed. and with an
afterword by Annalisa Cima and critical apparatus by
Rosanna Bettarini. Milan: Arnoldo Mondadori Editore. 1991.
Diario postumo: 66 poesie e altre. Ed. Annalisa Cima. Preface
by Angelo Marchese. Text and critical apparatus by Rosanna
Bettarini. Milan: Arnoldo Mondadori Editore, 1996.
L'opera in versi, ed. Rosanna Bettarini and Gianfranco Contini.
Turin: Giulio Einaudi Editore, 1980.
Il secondo mestiere: Arte, musica, società, ed. Giorgio Zampa.
Milan: Arnoldo Mondadori Editore, 1996.
Il secondo mestiere: Prose 1920–1979, ed. Giorgio Zampa. 2 vol-
umes. Milan: Arnoldo Mondadori Editore, 1996.

TRANSLATIONS OF MONTALE

Angelini, Patrice Dyerval, ed. and trans., *Poésies VII: Journal
posthume,* by Eugenio Montale. Paris: Editions Gallimard,
1998.
Ivo Barroso, trans., *Diário Póstumo,* by Eugenio Montale. Rio
de Janeiro: Editora Record, 2000.
Maria Ángeles Cabré, trans., *Diario póstumo, 66 poemas y
otras,* by Eugenio Montale. Introduction by Maria Ángeles
Cabré. Preface by Annalisa Cima. Barcelona: Ediciones de la
Rosa Cúbica, 1999.
Galassi, Jonathan, ed. and trans., *Collected Poems 1920–1954,*
by Eugenio Montale. Revised edition. New York: Farrar,
Straus & Giroux, 2000. [Includes *Ossi di seppia, Le occa-
sioni,* and *La bufera e altro*]
Galassi, Jonathan, ed. and trans., *Otherwise: Last and First
Poems of Eugenio Montale.* New York: Random House, 1984.
[Translation of *Altri versi*]

Galassi, Jonathan, ed. and trans., *The Second Life of Art: Selected Essays of Eugenio Montale*. New York: Ecco Press, 1982.

Koschel Christine, trans., *Die worte sprühen: Das postume Tagebuch 1*. Afterword by Annalisa Cima, with recollections of Montale by Carlo Emilio Gadda and Alberto Moravia. Munich: Peter Kirchheim Verlag, 1998.

OTHER WORKS

Atti del seminario sul Diario postumo di Eugenio Montale, Lugano, 24–26 ottobre, 1997. Second edition. Milan: All'Insegna del Pesce d'Oro, 1999.

Bernacchia, Monica. *Diario postumo di Eugenio Montale—il gioco, l'enigma e il dono (con "Indice ragionato" della critica)*. Unpublished dissertation, Università degli Studi di Urbino, Facoltà di Lettere e Filosofia, Corso di laurea in lettere moderne, Anno accademico 1997–1998.

Cima, Annalisa. *Repliche mai pubblicate dal "Corriere della Sera."* Milan: All'Insegna del Pesce d'Oro di Vanni Scheiwiller, 1999.

De Caro, Paolo. *Ludere pro eludere. Alcune agnizioni e qualche ipotesi a rischio per il cosidetto Diario postumo di Eugenio Montale*. Lugano: Annuario della Fondazione Schlesinger, 1994, 91–221.

Isella, Dante. *Dovuto a Montale*. Milan: Rossellina Archinto, 1997.

Marcenaro, Giuseppe. *Eugenio Montale*. Milan: Edizioni Bruno Mondadori, 1999.

Marchese, Angelo. *"L'autocitazione nel 'Diario postumo' di Montale. Otto/Novecento*, XX–XXI, 1996–1997, 143–166.

Marchese, Angelo (ed.). *Poesie* by Eugenio Montale. Milan: Arnoldo Mondadori Scuola, 1997.

Savoca, Giuseppe. *Concordanza del "Diario postumo" di Eugenio Montale. Facsimile dei manoscritti, Testo, Concordanza*. [Florence]: Leo S. Olschki Editore, 1997.